OLIVIER SAILLARD

An ABC of Hermès Crafts

ACTES SUD | HERMÈS

Such is the art
of small things
that change
everything,

with no other
"use" than
to please the eye
and hand.
O. S.

A CHANSON DE GESTES: such was the definition of Hermès proffered by a visitor being taken around the workshops one day. It is certainly a good description, for those who see the house "from within", of the humming, mysteriously busy hive that is the reality behind the famous signature. It is a "land of the hand", a country whose extent and variety of activity few could imagine. An incessant ballet of nimble fingers deftly working materials they master from start to finish. Building on the solid foundation of its savoir-faire as a saddle and harness maker, Hermès is now proficient in sixteen different types of activity. In these *métiers*, its artisans proceed as both experts and aesthetes, making saddles, garments, hats, shoes, bespoke shirts, printed silk, perfume, gloves, jewellery, watches, homeware and tableware – and to this list, which remains open, its fellow companies add the art of crystal, silver and boot-making. All their unique forms of expertise can in turn be broken down into series of specific operations, punctuated by dextrous, expert actions, precise and meticulous techniques that leave very little room for chance or hesitation. Oddly enough, while impossible to describe without the aid of a manual demonstration or diagram, many of these actions have their own accredited words to explain or at least to name them. This is the sign of a very old and very close partnership between doing and saying. It makes Hermès one of the great repositories of an original linguistic heritage. Words forged in the workshop, sometimes existing only within this closed circle and not even in the dictionary, familiar or almost esoteric, easily translated onomatopoeia, or syllables hermetic to all but initiates, a few of them rare or even lost, others freshly or naively invented, they form a distinct, rich and expressive vocabulary shaped by the long memory of artisanship, wearing the patina of use, revisited by the eccentricities of oral transmission, a thesaurus that is nectar for linguists, sociologists, poets and simply the curious.

Now, for the first time, at the initiative of Pierre-Alexis Dumas, the house's Artistic Director, Hermès is opening its book of *words of the tribe*, letting them speak, choosing to assemble some hundred verbs in the inventive and inspired prose of Olivier Saillard. From *abat-carrer* to *visiter*, via *bichonner, chipoter, décreuser*, *gratte-bosser*, *insculper*, *liéger*, *marier*, *palissonner, planer*, *putoiser*, *rétreindre*, *roulotter* and *sabrer*, this lover of language familiar with the innermost folds of fashion was given full latitude to play on incongruities, correspondences, shifts of meaning and syllogisms – and even the nonsensicality that is just begging to be noted (for example, when a leather worker adds a second lining the word is *doubler*, when it should logically be *tripler*, and when a gilder speaks of blocking he says he is striking – *frapper* – yet his hand is nothing if not gentle. These terms thus hold up a mirror to a surprising world. With intelligence, erudition, poetry, irony and tenderness, Olivier Saillard mixes anecdote and observation to offer us, rather than a portrait, a sum of details and of riches in the style of a pamphlet – a genial pamphlet, that is – on fashion, its practices and crafts. Like Voltaire's hero Candide, he invites us to be surprised.

MÉNÉHOULD DU CHATELLE[1]

1. Cultural Heritage Director, Hermès.

1

A

ABAT-CARRER

"This 'fini' which signals and signs the works of a French house is not obtained by high salaries. Only the friendly solidarity between the master and worker can pay and perpetuate it. We are old acquaintances, Emile Hermès and I. It is a pleasure to listen to this man of experience, up on the terrace that crowns his house. While warming my shoulders in the autumn sun, I learn from an expert mouth that loves its subject, I learn how Paris, abuzz with little noises, has worked unceasingly for the good name of Paris."[2]

Colette was on intimate terms with the professions of fashion and appearance. She was often the spokeswoman who, going beyond their fantastical facades, legitimised those modest or grand crafts that, like her readers, she esteemed.

For Hermès, for her friend Emile Hermès, she wrote these few lines that appeared in what at the time was not yet called a press kit. She delighted in the fact, as if in a character trait, that the famous leather maker lavished as much care on the underside as he did on the top of his distinguished creations. This determination to impart a "finish" even when it was

2. Text written by Colette for Hermès. Archives Hermès.

not visible is the music paper of the Paris workshops, whose score she so tenderly observed and described.

Abat-carrer is one of those actions that contribute to this silent, symphonic score, these skills that continue to make certain parts of the capital the conductor of serene fashions, the pole on which novelty is no more than a waving flag.

Abat-carrer consists in attenuating the sheer edge of a piece of leather in order to give it a rounded finish. Instead of abruptness, it gains in softness. Such is the art of small things that change everything, with no other "use" than to please the eye and hand.

ARRÊTER, STOPPING

Whatever the manner, whatever the skill involved, the process of making can lead along the most poetic paths. Technique does not despoil the subject, which remains pristine. Excellence can manifest itself in the almost negligible. In the visual arts, Robert Filliou elevated this principle to the expression of a style, making artistic manifestos out of a few scattered bits of wood, a few abandoned pieces of cardboard. "Art is what makes life more interesting than art", he said, his words magnifying the rudimentary tools of his creative process.

In fashion, such contradictions are not so fecund. When "faire" – making – dominates, to the detriment of "savoir-faire", the process is

often driven by the logic of an accelerated and absurd production system.
Hermès is no ordinary fashion label. It does not have the logo-laden profile of some schizophrenic bling merchant. Mastery is evident at every stage of making and each one is equal. It may be manifested in completion and even in a refusal.
For example, the way a seam is concluded is as worthy of the respect meted out to work well done as any other stage in the process leading to an object, bag or garment. There is not one final stitch, one full stop to bring the work to a halt. Rather, three back-tracking stitches done by hand will suffice and prevent unravelling. A hammer then helps these stitches joined by the permanence of the skill to recede into elegant discretion. The model, whether saddle or bag, no longer has a beginning or end. It simply, splendidly *is*.

ASTIQUER, POLISHING

"Hermès' greatest point of pride is in seeking to ensure that the underside equals the top, the inside the outside. Farewell flourishes, inlays, mannerism... A neat fastener, an ingenious buckle [...] is fine, quite fine enough."[3] With these simple words Colette paints the portrait of the French house. With fine movements, Hermès smoothes, polishes and rubs the edges

3. Text written by Colette for Hermès. Archives Hermès.

of leather. This unvarnished extravagance, a bit like a touch of liner or kohl beneath a pretty eye, consists in bringing a shine to the layer of leather.
In saddlery, this result is obtained after searing or buffing, colouring and drying, or by hand-rubbing the edges. The rag or round brush used here are replaced by a hot iron when it comes to polishing the edges of a belt. Bedecked with shadows for some, underscored by patience for others, the leather "yields a muffled cry under the rider",[4] caresses the hands, enlaces waists, punctuates figures: "Hermès continues".[5]

4. *Ibid.*
5. *Ibid.*

b

C

BICHONNER, CLEANING AND DRESSING

A fashion designer, apostle of modernity dressed in brushstrokes of black, was visiting the store-rooms of a costume museum. Flattered, the curator guided his steps through the centuries as they opened up before them in the form of hanging garments. These heavy embroidered tissues, this haute-couture taffeta, these ceremonial velvets, this socialite chiffon – how they wearied the vampire couturier.

It was quite a struggle for the curator in his grey flannel suit to wrest a smile from his guest. The protuberant dresses from the 1950s excited the museum man, but wearied the man of fashion. The splendour of a court coat and the exuberance of a finely wrought model did not especially fascinate the knowledgeable creator. The elevated exercise of haute couture struck him as vain exoticism.

Politely, he asked to see the functional pieces, the simplest and plainest of all. On seeing a worker's smock all covered with patches he allowed his admiration to show. Trousers shiny from a life of ironing sent him into raptures. He said he was deeply moved by the care and attention that still emanated from these "rough and ready" clothes and their thrifty owners.

He spoke at length about his nostalgia for "Sunday best", those clothes that were

respectfully folded away from one week to another.
Satisfied now, he took his leave.
Bichonner – cleaning and dressing– means taking care, applying the balm of equal consideration. To clean a shoe is to protect and embellish it. Using creams and beeswax, a broad brush or welt brush, applied wax, polish, one cleans, waxes and cossets a shoe, a belt, a chair or a bag.
It goes without saying, *bichonner* means preserving, scrubbing to make more lasting. Without a doubt, throwaway sentiments have no place here.

BRODER, EMBROIDERING
In the eighteenth century embroiderers were the object of the same covetous desires and graces as are couturiers today – and indeed, it was not until the fashion mongers came along that couturiers were seen as anything more than tailors.
At the risk of violent simplification, in this configuration antithetical to our present situation, the tailor (couturier) was the accredited supplier of the embroiderer! The relative stability of sartorial forms denied him the kind of freedom of expression afforded to the embroiderer. From the most discreet to the most flamboyant, embroidery defined the garment.
Not many fashion houses kept an embroidery department. Jeanne Lanvin did. She loved

exotic-style embroideries and insisted on having an in-house workshop. But the number of embroiderers shrank faster than the number of fashion houses. Rébé and Lesage, masters of haute couture, worked brilliantly to uphold their craft and counter, both nobly and humbly, their own status as contemporary subcontractors.

It would be pointless to look for equivalents at Hermès. As to out-and-out embroidery, there is little of that. It is to be found here only in its most secret version. The verb is claimed by artisans in the workshop for bespoke shirts. Here they embroider two details that are highly appreciated by connoisseurs: buttonholes and initials. Considered by some as fully-fledged embroidery, these call for a quality of attention praiseworthy both in its tenderness and its concentration.

Sewn on "a hidden placket imprinted with an iron", the proud buttonhole must negotiate the "pavements" formed by the obdurate thickness of necessary fabric and avoid "birds", as V-shaped cutting accidents are known.

Attentive and diligent, the artisans pin down other flying creatures, creatures that elsewhere they drive off, by sewing "swallows" (house-shaped pieces of fabric) which stabilise and strengthen the stitching of the shirt tails.

Synonymous with proper finishing and discretion, these embroideries are also the house signature written in *petit-point*.

C

r

CADRER UNE PEAU, FRAMING A SKIN

Leather is a subject. It is a theme or a figure of style which always comes to dominate those who use or wear it. As much as the form and function that define it, a leather blouson is also the skin that brutally identifies it, socially, musically and sensually.

Emile Hermès prided himself on the fact that each new development in the house took place exclusively under the sign of leather, and that saddlery was the aesthetic filter for each new department.

More than the material content, leather is a table of contents. In it we can read the whole history and evolution of a house that one day chose a waiting horse as its ex-libris.

To frame or stretch a skin might by respectful logic be taken to mean putting a skin in a frame, placing it at the centre, at the heart of noble pieces of wood that set off its prestige.

One could certainly look at it that way, for these skins stretched and held by metal clips are, in and for themselves, untouchable and untouched works of visual art. They are the introductions to new chapters that are all devoted to leather.

This framing corresponds to two stages and necessities. Before starting the process of tanning, the skins that arrive are wet, heavy and pungent. One way of preserving them is to dry them at under fifty degrees. The skins are then hung up like sheets of paper, pinned on frames in order to preserve their natural form. To obtain the suppleness and fine texture required, the tanned, coloured skins are then dried, massaged, thinned and wrung. Fulling will bring out their natural grain, just as in the world of stationery different kinds of paper have their specific weight. This process of straining stretches the skin and promises that the surface will soon be flatter than the pages of a book.

Making a bag, or a saddle, is thus a long epilogue whose title is Hermès.

CHIPOTER, QUIBBLING

One day in the 1970s a futuristic couturier peremptorily declared that "We are not here to do couture!" In his way he was contributing to the violent shift in the status of a figure who in the nineteenth century was a purveyor, and who by the 1960s had become a superstar. By denying the tools of his technique, this outspoken designer was inventing other methods. Some of which were virtuous, because technological. Others were less agreeable because based on new rules of marketing and promotion that shunted fashion into a syndrome involving the full-bore industrialisation of novelty. They put a label on the art of living and distributed it in department stores at knockdown prices.

In design studios, in offices and among journalists, there was quibbling aplenty. They cavilled shamelessly to justify the selling machine. Hemlines, colours and periods clashed at an ever more frantic rhythm.
At Faubourg Saint-Honoré this prattle was rebutted by the permanence of a creative discourse.
And when quibbling – *chipotage* – occurred in the house itself, there was nothing casuistic about it. At Hermès, *faire de la chipote* meant retouching those tiny flaws invisible to most eyes that occur in the printing of silk scarves.
Involving a succession of frames, each one for a different colour, printing sometimes produces anomalies. Some colours are "off-frame": the print is not applied in the right place, leading to the appearance of blanks that need to be filled by hand.
At Hermès, to quibble – *chipoter* – is to rectify. Not to add to the ambient blather.

CIRER, WAXING

In the photographs of August Sander agricultural labourers, notables, butchers and doctors pose for the camera in their working clothes or Sunday best.
The latter can be recognised by their crispness, the stiffness that contrasts with the floppy colours of the weekday uniforms. They also declare themselves by the starch we know is there and by the evidence of ironing attesting

the attention lavished on these plain ceremonial clothes.
Ordinary or elaborate, they bespeak the care people took over their outfits before fashion made this feeling unfashionable. Shiny from all the upkeep, as dandies at the end of the nineteenth century said they should be, the nobility of these clothes was revealed progressively with the effects of wear and care.
Applying wax to leather nourishes it and helps keep it in its original state as long as possible. The thread that the artisan uses to make the famous saddle stitch is also coated after rubbing with a cake of beeswax, guaranteeing solidity and permanence. This balm, covering even the linen thread, is not mere cosmetic flattery, but an accord reached with time and ordeals that are not feared.

CISELER, CHASING

Burin and hammer and chiselling tools are used by silversmiths and sculptors striving to make metal more delicate than lace. Several techniques lead to the motif. Using tracing paper the artisan reproduces the design on the object and prints it by means of hammer blows to the burin. He may also hammer the decoration from the back in order to create a relief on the front. In order to heighten the relief and the hollows he then goes back to the surface and deburs. But if the chaser's precise blows to the metal are mechanical, he also has the concision and patience of an embroiderer.

COLLECTIONNER, COLLECTING

There are learned types and enthusiasts who confuse collecting with adding, accumulating, counting or totalising. Other, more relaxed or amorous persons, associate it with conserving. There is a kind of collector who is driven by the concern to have the whole series. For these completists, exhaustiveness is the goal to be attained. This obsessive search for the missing object soon veers into pathology and transforms a passion into a frustration. Others amass, publish catalogues raisonnés and show their collection like ingots in a safe, following the price curves of art in parallel with those of the stock exchange.

At Hermès, they assemble. The prestigious and ordinary objects that constitute the museum on the third floor, sandwiched between the store and workshops, have the charm of a cabinet of curiosities, lending a deaf ear to the discourse of heritage collections. Each piece relates to Hermès activities although none was made by the house. The tricycle horse that belonged to the son of Napoleon III, the plans for Bonaparte's imperial carriage, eighteenth-century Japanese stirrups and Arab and Tibetan saddles were brought together by Emile Hermès. This museum without an entrance is more a poetic attic for pleasurable musing than a learned exhibition. Here one

also finds singular or everyday items, like the bag of a house checkout assistant, patched and handsome as a talisman.
Like an active oral memory, sartorial creations, accessories, silk scarves and even tools for which special affection is felt are all preserved in a department called "the conservatoire". In this place of study and research for anyone eager to know more about Hermès, objects keep alive the memory and presence of crafts, and the actions of the artists and creators who work constantly with the house.

COLORER, COLOURING
Boxes of pencils offer young schoolchildren a range of colours that goes from tan to brick red, from chalk white to jungle green. This chart of basic colours, said to reflect their tender years, tends to grow more complex when language gets involved, for nothing is more simple and yet more complex than describing a colour.
What should we make of the "repenting blue" evoked by Simone de Beauvoir? Must we add the milky white of a cloud in order to embody one? Is it far from that "Lanvin blue" on which the fashion house built its success? Is it close to a "yesterday blue" or "today blue"? Can the colours that nature provides constitute the definitive colour atlas that we all dream of? Have all the shades of flowers, from poppy to primrose, been recorded on paper?

The more colours we identify and invent, the more, it seems, we need to invent still more. To name them is to broach the difficulty of representing them. To date, more than seventy-five thousand colours have been specially created for the printing of Hermès silk scarves, from "box orange" to "wet sand beige". Once an artist or illustrator has executed his drawing in one set of tones, a team of colourists is tasked with presenting a variety of versions. Each silk scarf is produced in a dozen different harmonies. The work of the artisans responsible for creating colours according to the formulae laid down by the colourists is still done partly by hand. Colorants and vegetable gums used as binder bubble away archaically while the range of shades grows constantly, mirroring the moods of the day. Before we find that elusive "repenting blue", there is a good chance we will come to daring blue and then regrets blue.

COMPOSER, COMPOSING

The perfumer is like a conductor with an orchestra. His nose does the work of the baton. The musicians that perform for him in the pursuit of his task are these two hundred-odd bottles of abstract raw materials placed on the carrousel that is their orchestra pit. In bringing together several fragrances, the perfumer composes. It may not always be useful to force them together or overdo the scoring. Sometimes a violin and a piano are all it takes

to turn a new smell into the most seductive piece of olfactory chamber music. Other perfumes, however, are the product of a mass of notes or musicians which give the big formations their power.
Jean-Claude Ellena, who presides over the creation of Hermès perfumes, concocts scents that are complete but not finished, like those haunting strains, those sonatas we hear one summer evening and that haunt us for days on end.

CONSIGNER, RECORDING

Ever since 1900 the saddle workshop under the eaves at 24 rue du Faubourg-Saint-Honoré, Paris, has kept bound registers. Covered with anonymous leather, they serve to record the history and production date of every horse saddle taken there for repair. Following an almost museum-like logic, the descriptions are organised thus: name of the craftsman, size of the client, measurements of the saddle, leather used, number, date of manufacture.
Fearing neither words nor the past, this system makes it possible to date many saddles that, having lived several lives with different owners, return to the workshops of the Faubourg for a subtle spot of beauty treatment.
Like a veritable ID card, a passport going back in time, the registers reiterate, page after page, year after year, the identification number stamped on the flaps of each saddle. Kept free from the tyranny of the present, alien to the

excesses of the contemporary, they are without equivalent, except perhaps the order books for haute couture clients.

However, no garment seems noble enough to preserve not only the mark of the person who conceived it, but also the labels and nail marks of all those who owned it. How calm and rested fashion would be if rid of its status as stillborn.

Fashion, that great amnesiac whose nature it is always to look to the future in luxury rear-view mirrors, could then give way to clothing.

COUCHER LES FONDS, LAYING THE GROUND

A little black dress, a bright red polo-neck sweater, blue jeans, an iron grey flannel skirt, a white shirt, a flower skirt, a putty-coloured trench coat…

There is a collective sartorial unconscious that makes certain kinds of clothes converge with certain colours, quite independently of fashion, which seeks to pervert this visual rightness. To recognise it is not to yield to a naïve or tired minimalism, but, on the contrary, to avoid the manias of aestheticism and retain only the elementary, which, throughout the twentieth century, has offered a much more bearable and wearable solution, sometimes even for the eccentrics who exhumed it.

"Laying the ground" is a basic action whose very simplicity will define an aesthetic approach for those enamoured of lessness and its method.

It is something that couturiers should learn, even if this laying of the ground is not directly applicable to the fields of fashion and textiles. It is a technique that concerns block-printed wallpaper. On a strip of paper ten metres long, the craftsman applies his chosen paint using two brushes in a choreography of eight interweavings in a way that makes for a homogenous ground and colour. Next, he takes a broad brush and applies big, peremptory strokes horizontally and then vertically. The paints and mixtures are identical and immutable: distemper, pigments, rabbit-hide glue, water. Once the ground is dry, the motifs are applied one by one, each having its own wooden block. We can wager that a designer, if compelled to use such practices, would draw from these sublime monochromes the essential that is also the divine superfluity we call the art of fashion.

COUDRE, STITCHING

"I love to knit jersey stitch. I knit, thinking half-thoughts. Or I bring emptiness and monotony to my empty, monotonous hours as I throw the thread between the needles, the seven days of my week are dispatched, I have lived them out on steel. I see my life extended with thousands of points. Yesterday, today, tomorrow – warm woollens. I touch, I enclose time."[6] Anyone who can appreciate these few

6. Violette Leduc, *La Chasse à l'amour*, Paris, Gallimard, 1973.

lines by Violette Leduc eagerly anticipating the moment when she can remove the ring of paper from around the balls of wool will be able to appreciate the quality of a stitch, a hem or a border. Perfect because uniform, sublime in its self-repetition, couture attains quality when the succession of stitches, one after another, veers towards a dizzying monotony.
Hand-stitching concerns a considerable part of the work done on Hermès saddles and leather goods. Saddle stitch is more like a signature. A compass and clamp serve to determine the holes to be pierced in the leather. The saddler's awl performs this task. A stitching clamps the pieces together. The artisan holds the pieces to be assembled between his knees. Using a length of thread called a *brassée* – an armful – its ends threaded through two needles, making movements like a swimmer, the artisan sticks in his arrows, interweaves, stretches his arms, pulling the thread along until he has delicately drawn the constant line of linen in its obediently inclined stitches.

COUPER, CUTTING

In the hierarchy of tasks and operations that lead to a garment or bag, houses and workshops proceed with respect for the strict rules of stitching.
By this we mean the act of stitching by hand, complementary to machine stitching. We linger lovingly for hours on the sewing that

some docile robe must have suffered. We acclaim embroidery as a feat both technical and stylistic. Sometimes the making time of a dress is touted as if its beauty was a consequence of the time it took. We forget that there are also humble clothes, industrially stitched, but sound in conception and execution.

We may acclaim the cut of a dress or coat, we are slower to distinguish the "cutter", the maker, than we are the couturier. But to whom is credit most due for the excellence of the garment? The inventive volume of sleeve invented by Cristobal Balenciaga and traced on a canvas, or its fine stitching? Which would be most justified in signing a handkerchief dress by Madeleine Vionnet? The elementary forms cut flat or the discreet stitches in the chiffon?

To cut is to make manifest a formal concept; stitching is a matter of shaping its form. Neither can manage without the other, even at its most rudimentary, for proportions, those famous proportions, come into play. Though absent from the language of today's fashion, they remain pernicious, transforming a woman into a figure of disconcerting excess or a tissue-paper silhouette. "A beautiful woman is one who is discreet, does not draw attention to herself", said Madame Grès, who always strove to alter the proportions of each model for clients so as not to disrupt the bodily harmony.

For leather goods, cutting requires a similar discipline. Often, the template around which forms are traced, a form that seems unchanging, will have been through several incarnations, several hesitant efforts towards an idea brought to maturity and one day fully achieved. The cutter must have a keen eye and a clever hand when the skin arrives. He is responsible for placing to optimal effect the different pieces of the puzzle that before the day is out will be a bag ready to hold forth. At Hermès, the cut is centred, which means that they "eat more skin". The secondary pieces may be used for smaller items such as watch-straps, diaries or small leather goods. Done by hand, using a metal tip and webs, by scissors too, but also on the machine, cutting must respect the grain of the skin and make the most of its natural flaws.

CRÉER UNE COMPLICATION,
CREATING A COMPLICATION

We spontaneously associate Hermès with horses and leather.

We give less thought to time as the constant material that the house has regularly and tenaciously embraced. Time, which propels other fashion houses into a marathon searching for the future, which makes them whinny and run at a gallop whenever the shadow of the past impinges on their brand, is tamed here like a fabric.

Whether dwelt upon or tracked down, in each workshop it is visibly appreciated.

Whether in the patina of leather of a well-preserved bag handed down from one generation to the next, or in the famous diaries, it can be seen that, here again, time floats free of the laws of hot-headed and over-the-top fashion.
At Hermès the tradition of watchmaking dates back to the 1920s, when the saddle-maker's talent was displayed in watches with skilfully crafted leather straps. By setting a fob watch in a piece of harness leather for one of his daughters, Emile Hermès prefigured the watchstrap, among other elegant innovations. Belt-watches, pocket watches, mechanical watches, sports and travel watches are as famous today as the bags created in the Faubourg workshops that epitomise the house's leather work.
In the field of watchmaking, a complication is an added function, something on top of the display of hours and minutes. It can be astronomical (moon phases, equation of time, etc.), technical (date, stop seconds) or practical (chronograph, *grande sonnerie*, alarm, repetition of minutes). The accumulation of mechanisms in the cramped space of the case adds to the watch's complexity and signals the watchmaker's great savoir-faire. Among the many models in this field, there is one at Hermès that is more chic and arrogant than any invention of fashion. By simply pressing a push-button, the hands of the *Arceau* watch, in its new *Le Temps suspendu* incarnation, stand still at an impossible hour and the date disappears until you

decide to restart time. All that remains to be tamed is silence, the kind that endures "like a fabric being torn."[7]

CUEILLER

Using a gathering or blowing iron, the glassmaker takes up the quantity of crystal that he can use to make a parison (the original form of the glass, but also the upper part from which we drink: the head). He takes small quantities for a stem or foot (the foot, logically enough, is what the glass rests on, and the stem connects it to the parison).

This singular vocabulary, which only glassmakers really master, should not put us off. To entertain readers, glassblowers have invented a more fanciful lexicon in which we find the verb *cueiller.*

At Saint-Louis, as at other manufactories, *cueiller* means gathering on the end of one's iron the material needed to make a glass or decanter. *Cueiller* is not to be confused with *cueillir*, to pick. As the glassmakers say, to the delight of poetic souls, *cueiller* is to crystal as *cueillir* is to cherries.

7. "Le silence dura comme une étoffe qu'on déchire." Louis Aragon, *Aurélien*, Paris, Gallimard, 1944.

D

DÉCOMPOSER, BREAKING DOWN

The great virtue of time is that it leads us step by step towards an exemplary quality of execution, a prospect made ever more remote by the extreme contemporariness of today's world. It would seem that the slow procedures implicit in making a bag or silk scarf are there to ensure the solidity of the idea. It is nice to think that because of all the consideration and handling lavished on it the nascent object here is not really "new" in the sense understood elsewhere. In this respect it has exactly the same quality that a dandy cherished in the late nineteenth century: unique, fresh to the world, and without the cellophane mirage of newness. Making a silk scarf is such a time-consuming task, with so many different exercises to carry off, that it cannot allow itself to pander to the illusions of fashions that flare up, dazzle and suddenly fizzle out. It is as if the time of making was not enough to test the document being prepared – hence the decision to deconstruct it as well. This is the phase which consists in breaking down the design of the silk scarf. This concerns the engraving process required to print the chosen design by means of frames. Each shot or transparency corresponds to a frame that itself corresponds to a colour that is printed. The engraver will thus break down the original drawing into what is a kind of backwards storyboard of single images, without risking failure. He is the maker of a film on canvas, applying his talent back to front. Just when the *carré*, the silk scarf, seems finished, it must be broken down into chapters. One by one, in Indian ink, the different values of shades and tones are transferred onto transparencies. The charm of the visible sequences derives from their fidelity to the original model and subject. A *carré* is not simply a stylistic contraction between illustrator and designer. It is the repository of the minutiae of crafts performed by those who brought it to fruition. Even when the motifs that once cast their guise over their era have fallen out of fashion, a foulard from Hermès is never cast aside. For it is not merely the memory of its wearer but the inextinguishable torchbearer of those who made it.

DÉCREUSER, DEGUMMING

Our endlessly revived habit of consumption and the abundance of sartorial designs have placed clothing and appearance at the heart of our daily experience. For more than half the planet, clothing is no longer a privilege. There are so many inexpensive garments that they have become a natural right, causing us to lose sight of the industrial or artisanal process leading to their existence. A visit to a garment workshop, whether its production is limited or mass-market, changes the way we think about the inhabitants of our wardrobe.

Just imagine, if we suddenly had to make our own clothes again, our second skin costumes, what rough and ready, probably shapeless costumes we would have to put up with! Now we can better appreciate the value of ready-to-wear in the twentieth century, which seriously simplified but also democratised our clothing, whose quality, everyone now agrees, is a thousand times superior to that of the workaday clothes with which a large percentage of the population had to make do before the 1960s.
Superior clothing should not turn us into walking financial scandals but proudly bear witness to a balance – flouted elsewhere – between quality and stylistic and creative options. Discreet or showy, it must confirm a precise pedigree that makes it a rarity.
The rudimentary cut of a scarf no doubt makes it the simplest accessory in a woman's wardrobe. Yet it too bears a passport stamped with operations that are far from negligible.
Three months separate the arrival of the raw silk, harvested according to traditions that respect the breeding of silk worms, and the production of the rolls of twill that frame-printing will turn into the famous Hermès scarves. For half a century now, their silk has been spun exclusively by Les Tissages Perrin.
Several transformations are essential to making a scarf, including winding onto spools the skeins of raw, natural-coloured silk, thick and sheathed in sericin, a kind of natural glue secreted by the silk worm. Spinning is another

important operation. It produces the famous twill, which can be recognised by the serge-like weave with fine, diagonal ribs that endows it with great stability. Degumming is an intervention that consists in washing the fabric in soap made from olive oil, in order to dissolve the sericin. As a result, the fabric loses a third of its weight and can now be ironed. Print-framing, the true work of "illumination", can now begin.

DEMANDER, REQUEST

At the turn of the twentieth century, Hermès excelled at making dog leashes and collars that turned elegant lady walkers green with envy. In around 1927, the house's first belts were inspired by these handsome collars. At the request of a couturière, Marie Gerber, one of the three directors of Callot Sœurs, these leather lengths made to go round the necks of pooches were adapted to the waists of haute couture clients. This project, considered eccentric at the time, was entrusted to the special orders workshop.

Housed in the hive at Faubourg Saint-Honoré, this workshop of busy virtuoso artisans still caters to every request, even the most far-fetched, providing they cultivate the art of singularity and uniqueness.

DESSINER, DRAWING

Drawing is more than a verb; when it serves noble practices and enters the realm of design,

it is an art. It is present on every floor of the workshops and design studios, and its meaning is more or less sophisticated or technical depending on its environment and field of application.
For women and men's ready-to-wear, it would seem that it is all about restraint. This reserve is the essence of a style that is always just right and never goes out of fashion.
Some design for the times, others for people – that seems to be the message here. Like an historian of clothing afflicted with myopia, whose memory holds only the unaltered archetypes of apparel that changes imperceptibly, clothing designers at Hermès seem to draw on and magnify a collective sartorial unconscious. Down with the excess of styles that makes garments loud and verbose, here they are required to say only the essential. A long dress declares its identity without the need for artifices that will shorten its life.
Designing also means learning to draw less. This striving for restraint, a restraint that is not prudence, generates a stylistic framework, an array of apparel that is classical because it is modern.
There is a place where design has other, applied characteristics. A measured use is made of it in creating the famous silk scarves, the *carrés*. In this case, designing means drawing. The motifs and themes may change, but never the protocol. The theme is known two years beforehand.

Illustrators, like hunters without guns, set their sights on forms, landscapes and colours, and work assiduously to produce a drawing in the 90 x 90 cm format that will soon be enrolled as a scarf.
The team at the design studio work on small stools made of plain wood, as they have for decades. Putting their drawings on the floor, they talk composition, "activate the diagonal", discuss the "handle", the shadows, and suggest a baptismal name. The scarf can be sent to Lyon for engraving, where it will be broken down into successive frames.
No prohibitions, no constraints are imposed on the illustrators. Furthermore, all are capable of respecting a methodology whereby the drawing begins at the centre of the square and moves out towards the corners, for it is these tips that are the scarf's most visible and looked-at parts when it is worn over the shoulder.
There is one self-imposed principle: not to represent sharp objects or cutting edges – quite simply, they don't want to prick the neck.
At Hermès, designing means a light, caressing touch.

DONNER SA MAIN, GIVING HANDLE
Like those endless little figures in paper cut-outs, linked arm to arm, the workshops at Hermès are connected by the hand. It is everywhere, whether in everyday, factual or poetic language. "Giving one's hand", however, does

not mean accepting a wedding ring. There is no serious allusion here to marriage, even if we can detect a language of amorous attachment between worker and house, between the artisan and his or her craft.

After a series of stages, the skin becomes leather thanks to the intervention of tanners who work to bring out its grain, its colour, its suppleness – its "handle".

A piece of leather "gives its handle" or "hand" in the sense that it combines suppleness and perfection of the skin. This is something you can feel by the repeated practice of touching and handling. "Having hand", it so happens, is an expression used to designate leather that is firm, strong, and impeccable in appearance. Leather is beautiful, they say at Hermès, when it "returns your caress". Whatever the word chosen, on the tip of the tongue or from the tips of the fingers, the answer is always embodied. Within arm's reach, at arm's length, leather is always intimately bound to the confident hand. Even the good old generic term "handbag" takes on a special meaning here, one that is modest, personal and rare.

DOUBLER, LINING

There is something even more intimate than clothing. Lining's relation to the body is even closer. It is the dark or coloured shadow of jackets. It is a protective balm between the skin it watches over and the dryness of certain fabrics

that it rebukes with some of its caresses, and that it coaxes, too.
When clothes reach a point of collapse, acclaimed by the wind and squalls of gazes, the demure lining remains immured, taking care to appear only furtively, precisely at the moment when no one is talking about it.
Couturiers cultivate fields sown with little flowers, a parterre of petals, in the jackets they fashion. Usually they cut leaden skies, cropped meadows and incessant rains in satin or warming twill. Even more plainly, a few pale stripes crisscross a hesitant whiteness on which no words will ever be written.
At Hermès a man's jacket can be lined, half-lined or unlined. In such cases, the operations carried out by hand call for special attention when it comes to the inner pockets, the piping and the strengthening under the arms. Trousers, likewise, are caressed down to the knee by their twin, a hidden under-part in strict cotton or satin. Some overcoats, trench coats or blousons are also fully lined with lambskin. Silk and cashmere are the vital supporting cast for gloves that would be mute without them. Among leather goods, lining and second-lining add the solemnity and seriousness signally lacking in the faker's wares. They are in lambskin, goatskin or other leathers, making the hand feel that it is sliding into a nest of lavished care. Sometimes the garment is self-lined, for even more discretion and

absence, for more distinction, so as to offer a garment for the gaze and another for the wearer, and no one else.

DRESSER, LAYING-OFF

Some garments more than others are the sculptures of those who wear them. Even limp, still orphaned, they are the poetic negatives, back-to-front states of the body, still to come. The concertina folds of a trouser leg that fell at the foot of the bed lead to happiness if one is lying with the person who will slip into them and, conversely, to despair, if they have just left.

Shoes and gloves, too, possess a degree of power over their master. Emptied, they still retain a degree of autonomy. Unlike suits or dresses that eventually collapse, they never go limp. This is obvious in the case of shoes, whose volume rests on a foundation, a flat sculptural form appreciated by men and women for centuries. And it is, too, with gloves, for they are no doubt the most anthropomorphic form of apparel. Whether in soft or more rigid leather, a glove fits, well, like a glove. Fresh from the workshop, it is placed on a warm metal hand on which it is adjusted, stretched, smoothed, positioned and arranged until it becomes this negative or positive double that is more faithful than the five fingers. This, in workshop parlance, is what they call the technique of laying-off.

Γ

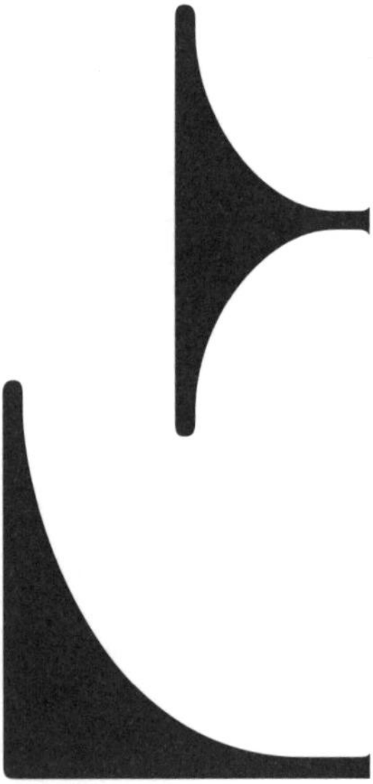

EMPAQUETER, PACKAGING

The ready-to-wear industry has replaced the refined couture house box with the insolent shopping bag, and protective tissue paper with a hygienic sheet of plastic. Few great names of fashion have maintained the use of those thick cardboard boxes into which a garment is gently eased. Hermès is one of them. It certainly does not neglect its containers, all those different kinds of boxes that some even collect for their own sake.

At Cristalleries Saint-Louis, *empaqueter* has an even more definitive meaning. It has to do with the making of paperweights. If this has anything to do with packaging, then the material is clear crystal rather than crumpled paper. To make a paperweight, sticks of equal length must be accumulated and assembled vertically in a metal mould. They are heated and then the glassmaker covers them with clear crystal so that they can be removed from the mould. Placed in the oven, welded together like Siamese twins, the rods are then flattened before being packed into the noblest and most chic wrapping of all: clear crystal, which does battle with wind and disorder in our offices.

ENNOBLIR, ENNOBLING

The quest for beauty can turn into an obsession and become neurasthenic when compounded by the syndrome of novelty. Was it not perplexing to hear a compulsive couturier repeating the same announcement with great aplomb at the start of each season, hailing the arrival of a modern collection that looked to the past and yet was resolutely of the present? Did we not frown and dare consternation when seeing that the evidence said the opposite?

Seeking out beauty is a bit like hunting for fish: some are patient anglers, others prefer to stick a net in a pool of farmed salmon.

Beauty is much more simple to access. To speak its name is tantamount to tracking it down. All you gather is the reflection of a style.

I believe that beauty is never spoken about flagrantly in any Hermès workshop. They are more likely to evoke nobility, the seriousness of the métiers, respect and quality, at the risk of making beauty sound like the affectation of a girl caked in make-up.

In the same spirit, they talk of *ennobling* silk scarves. This refers to the finishing operations, notably dyeing and printing, which complete and sign the scarf. Fixing the colours, washing, flat-drying, cutting and rolling with silk thread are the final stages. If they do not speak the beauty that the scarf thirsts for, they do make it possible to circumscribe the grace of the beauties who will soon display it around their necks.

ESTAMPILLER, STAMPING

On every floor, whether lined with textiles or leather, the artisan stamps, embosses, signs and attests his intervention for eternity. Porcelain is no exception. Each piece is signed on the back with the stamp, the seal of the collection, motif or colour chosen for the occasion, and the sign of the artisan who decorated it. Primacy goes to the signature of the workshop and house. No concession is ever made to the logo-logorrhoea that transforms precious and meticulous savoir-faire into an advertising pitch.

ÉTIRER, STRETCHING

At Saint-Louis the *millefiori* crystal paperweight is a multicoloured glass ball which looks as if it was picked in a field of flowers and is placed like a hostage on our green paper thoughts. *Millefiori* are the result of cutting and joining rods of crystal in different motifs and colours. They originate with the melting of a cylinder of crystal. Two steel tubes fixed at the ends stretch it to the degree required. This manual, choreographic operation is the work of master glassmakers who, tube in hand, eye to eye, stretch the crystal by moving further apart from each other. There are fifteen or twenty metres between them when the boiling cylinder becomes the desired fine, thin rod. In a long wooden gutter, it slowly cools before being cut into lengths. It is the bits and fragments, the broken memories of fragile rods, that will soon be used to weight down flighty folders.

FAÇONNER

Only silk is *façonné*. This enigmatic word does not hide a privilege or special consideration but a technique applied to the world of ties. Since 1949, when the manager of the Cannes store, Bobby Breward, had the idea of providing a Hermès tie to facilitate access to the neighbouring casino for his clients, the brand has offered models in woven silk. This "heavy silk" tie, as it is also called, can be recognised by the way its motifs are obtained from a weave made with threads of different colours. The nuances of relief and texture will depend on the way the threads cross the weave. These are what distinguish the "heavy silk" from the twill tie. As does another singularity: it is made up of three pieces rather than two: neck, blade and tail.

Self-lined, signed with an H, woven and then dyed, the *façonné H* tie is a monochrome pictogram, one among the house's many, constantly renewed designs.

FERMER, FASTENING

The history of clothes and fashion can also be told in terms of dressing. The act of putting on clothes. For the actions and movements pertaining to this process differ from one century or decade to the next.

In the eighteenth century, two ladies-in-waiting were needed to lace and fasten corsets and organise the folds of a hoop skirt.
In the nineteenth century there was much lacing, buttoning and clipping, and these many delicate actions requiring the help of a man transformed the woman's garment into a taffeta prison.
In its paradoxical accession to modernity and withdrawal into its past, the twentieth century multiplied simplifying procedures leading to the contemporary garment. It freed women who, like men, could now dress themselves alone.
They zipped, buttoned and unbuttoned freely, using press studs, Velcro and elastic. As clothes softened and became a genuine second skin, so they were slipped on rather than put on. Once long and drawn-out, dressing was reduced to a quick, sporty action. The uniforms of modernity that are the Chanel black dress, that minimalist manifesto first issued in 1927, the sports outfit that Hermès helped to democratise, and Rykiel's soft pullovers and trousers, which imposed a new physical approach, did more to renew and transform fashion than any new stylistic invention.
Among these revolutions, there is one that Hermès cannot disown. Emile Hermès called it the "American fasten-all". The zipper was brought to France and given currency there by the famous house on the Faubourg. After

travelling out to North America on a mission for the French cavalry in 1914, Emile Hermès came back from Canada with a sliding system that equipped the hood of the automobile he had been travelling around in. He obtained exclusive rights and became one of its pioneering users in France after the war. From the military to the civilian, and from industry to artisanship, this "lightning" fastener (which is why the French for zip is *fermeture éclair*) lent itself to many new uses. It posed on a famous bag, later renamed the *Bolide*, and brought movement to the sporty clothes of which Hermès was the outstanding maker from the 1920s onwards. Its name an onomatopoeia sounding like something out of a Futurist manifesto, the zip has been inseparable from the way we dress ever since the 1930s. Less obsolete than any other clothing feature, it is a metal movement and metallic noise that has never been rejected. And that is no doubt why Emile Hermès used to say that his "he started to loosen up clothing by using a new fastener."

FEUILLETER, LEAFING THROUGH

There is still a world of unlikely professions that continue to exist in this contemporary world of ours. Extravagant and yet recorded in the register of trades, they excite and exceed our imagination with their unexpectedness. At Hermès, a *feuilleteuse* is the person who examines the famous diaries before they are given their store baptism and, later, submit to the diktat of our pens. Page after page, she skilfully dispenses with any unwanted blemishes, checks the articulation, the spiral, and assesses the pattern of our future lives with a kindly eye.

It is a trade. It is also the beginning of a novel. "The pages of the diary have been printed, folded, cut, perforated on the back and on the thumb notches, then pressed, buffed, gilded and rounded, their corners given a last coat of gold with a gilding pad, and finally set in a metal binding."[8] Every morning, the *feuilleteuse* took in hand the blank future that would soon be put on sale. She verified the solvency of the pages and the phantom lives that she momentarily possessed and did not doubt that, in her hands, hours and days that for now were ordinary would soon cease to be so.

FEUTRER, RUBBING WITH FELT

Dandies saw the new as the excessive reflection of fashion. They favoured neutrality and the chic of a seemingly worn garment. The most dogged among them even went to far as to rub their suits with fragments of glass so as to bestow the noble lustre that today we tolerate only on denim and leather. One of them proudly sported a carefully damaged coat that had the lacy texture of a cobweb.

8. Sophie Chérer, *Monde d'Hermès* 57, "Feuilleter", p. 28.

At Hermès, the point of rubbing is to change the appearance of a skin. Tanned and dyed leather is rather matt. It is possible to change its relief and brilliance, and even to confer a shine that is almost mirror-like. Some of them are vigorously polished with an agate stone or a block of glass. Just as Moroccan tadelakts are polished with pebbles, Hermès uses stones on its crocodile and lizard skins and polishes its Boxcalf.
Other skins – the delicate lamb, enigmatic emu, insolent ostrich and still avid crocodile – are rubbed with wool felt. Simply corrupted and polished (*astiqués*), others play the palimpsest. They then acquire a satiny patina that can look quite surprising. Our dandies of centuries past would have approved.

FONDRE, CASTING
Standing in front of window displays where the artifices of fashion turn must-haves, some clients swoon, others melt with happiness and desire. Some are unable to resist and simply crack. What these insatiable *élégantes* most often melt for, jewellery, is itself created using a technique that itself involves melting: the melting in lost wax casting.
As when making sculptures, a rubber mould is made using a metal model. In this a wax copy is cast. A plaster mould is then created around the wax. The jewel is obtained by flowing molten metal into the mould. The metal

pushes out and replaces the wax. Once it has cooled, the plaster mould is shattered and frees the gold or silver jewel. Gracefully displayed on velvet chokers, visible to all, chains and bracelets berate passers-by, casting without warning their happy spell on future round necks.

FRAPPER – DORER SUR CUIR, PRINTING – GILDING LEATHER

Milliners started marking their name on the inside of their hats when they were fed up with mending models brought back to their workshop by negligent clients who, it often turned out, had bought them elsewhere. Hence labels.

Couturiers and then designers marked their creations in order to fight against the copiers but also to sign clothes whose aesthetic ambitions gradually won recognition. These "artists working in the medium of dresses" outdid each other in imagining singular ways of signing. Handwritten signatures woven on ribbons, as if they had fallen to the bottom of a canvas, were placed on the waist. Subtle logos by Thayat and Cassandre doubled up along the edge of fabrics. Madeleine Vionnet left a fingerprint like a suspect at the police station. One student couturier event went so far as to call himself Griffe, Jacques Griffe – like the designer's mark: a *griffe*.

Later on, the client's monogram started to disappear, replaced by scattered initials that made bags and clothes schizophrenic.
At Hermès, leather is imprinted – *frappé*. And, using gilding stamps, it is gilded. The artisan delicately presses the stamp down on the leather in order to obtain a burned, tone-on-tone effect, then comes back to the gold leaf. Knock, knock? Who's there? Hermès. Hermès who? Hermès Paris, Made in France. Can I come in?

C

I

GAINER, CASING

The art of casing is at its most consummate when we can no longer tell which is the negative and which the positive, which the case and which the object housed. Which is the hollow, which the full form? The apple case, a mini-bag in lambskin the colour of a Granny Smith with an interior structure made by the silversmith Puiforcat, and the real apple that will soon make it its home, are not rivals. The latter's beauty is marvellously reflected in the virtuoso receptacle of the other. Casing techniques are all inspired by saddle-making and apply the same finishes as leather work. There is no limit to their applications, even if for leather this is a world of heightened constraints. Upholstery for cars, music cases, pieces of furniture and boxes of every kind have all found, one day, their twin in coloured or natural skin in the workshops dedicated to that cause. If the artisan redoubles his efforts and tricks of the trade to fit the leather as closely as he can to the object to be *cloned*, then it is for the client to observe the almost perfect regularity of the hand-stitching, which is also the signature of authenticity, the signature of the always unique work.

GLACER, GLAZING

Mannered because of all their expensive preparations, fashion photographs have transformed glossy paper into glacial images. This deformation does not belong to the present only. As early as the 1930s, artistic directors and couturiers loved to portray the draped beauties of the period as Hollywoodian marble masks immortalised in black and white. These perfect, slick fashion pages fascinate by their immobility. Retouched, they offer not only a sartorial dream, but also a version of an ideal world that is not always close to life. The natural is at home here only when decreed to be an artifice in the same way as an accessory. Even when naked, a woman is already dressed. Still lifes can crop up where not expected. A Mexican photographer, Enrique Metinides, produced an image at the intersection of these ideas while not strictly working for fashion. In a photo from 1979, Adela Legarreta Rivas, a journalist at the height of her beauty, is seen in repose like a shop-window dummy, with blood dripping from her lips in a manner later occasionally used by Guy Bourdin. The story behind this image is more disturbing. That day, the journalist in the photograph was leaving her beautician after having had her nails and hair done, and decided to walk to the venue where she was holding a press conference for the publication of her new book. On the way she was hit by a white Datsun and

killed at once. The photographer, who specialised in reportage, accidents and miscellaneous news, did a proper job. The image was seen around the world, covered by the thin transparent shroud of glossy magazines. It must be admitted, fashion can send a chill down your spine. These skinny bodies, these slaves of appearance, these hollow cheeks and high heels are not the joyous depiction of an age. The vain pages of fashion mags are not the only places where gloss is loved. People love the shine on shoes, macs or bags, and sometimes immerse themselves in vinyl or everything-plastic.
At John Lobb, all the waxing and buffing lavished on a shoe described as glazed makes it a shiny mirror, the dizzying image of our times.

GRATTE-BOSSER, BUMP-SCRATCHING
The bump-scratcher is a curiosity of the kind that are plentiful in the trades of fashion and appearance. And yet there are few lumps to be scratched away here. At a stretch perhaps one may find counter forms that propose new silhouettes by re-shaping the body. Bump-scratching has nothing to do with relieving an itch – nor is it worth getting the hump over. To be clear, it could be a case of you scratch mine I'll scratch yours, except that at Hermès the only one who gets rubbed up the right way is the horse and that's no hollow quid pro quo. And bump-scratching is of no help in that kind of flattery.

Its function is very different. The bump-scratcher is a tool in fibreglass, a kind of large brush with dense hairs that is used to apply a satiny surface to gold. It is valued for the decoration of porcelain change trays, for example. A charming and old fashioned tool, the bump-scratcher will, if you knock it with your bonce, rap but not hurt.

GRAVER, ENGRAVING

In 1948 a meeting between the engraver Marcel Gandit and the printer Auguste Arnaud determined a new future for Hermès scarves, which had been created the decade before. The so-called "flat-frame" or "Lyonnais frame" technique allowed a significant increase in the number of colours. It was also conducive to great quality and variety of designs. A frame consists of a piece of gauze stretched and blocked except at those points where the colour must be let through, and a metal structure to hold it. But without the engraver's art the iron frame would remain cold and distant. When the drawing for a silk scarf reaches him in the form of a full-size model, hand-drawn, his role is to break it down, one frame per colour. With Indian ink for lines and fine contours, and gouache for patches, each colour is handled individually on a transparent piece of film. Breaking down a design with thirty colours takes four hundred to six hundred hours of engraving. This long, industrial and creative process combines traditional skills of the kind that the cradle of the Lyonnais silk industry can still offer, as well as other forms of competence arising directly from craft, where the artisan excels by dexterity and also patience.

GRIFFER, MARKING

One fine day, fashion decided to leave its claw-mark in clothes that had always been anonymous. Asserting their feline force throughout the twentieth century, these woven or printed *griffes* – labels – were far from bland and inoffensive. They enliven collars and enchant waists but can also annoy, irritate and scratch the skin. Their intentions have been so imperious that, having made themselves omnipresent and invasive, their arrogance is no longer needed: if they disappeared, people would only clamour to have them back. Even when naked, tanned, plucked and muscle-toned, our rectified body is already labelled by fashion, which acts on the epidermis as well as on its envelope.

Hermès does not do *griffes*. It suggests its presence. The artisan who applies a *griffe* here is using a tool to bite into the leather and mark the spots required for the famous Hermès saddle stitch. This instrument, a kind of comb with teeth spaced differently for each type of operation, is used to guide the needle and thus ensure the regularity that makes a finer signature than any flashy logo.

GUILLOCHER, CHECKERING

For some, a watch is a reminder that is disguised on the wrist in the form of a dial and a strip of leather. Just as people used to tie a knot in their handkerchief (when such things were still in cotton!), so now they fasten around their arms these personal clocks that we both maintain and avoid.

The mobile phone, PDA and pocket computer have all failed to dethrone the watch, that historical vestige of time mastered by obligation and fantasy. For the watch is a piece of jewellery, an ornament. Its look is the surest means of saving from obsolescence a movement invented long ago, even when its results are inconstant.

Hermès watches stand out by their simplicity but are no less complex and sophisticated for all that. Whether the models are for sporting or city wear, for the pocket or stylish and/or bohemian, they bear witness to a tradition that winds back to the 1920s and has always combined simplicity and refinement.

In the Swiss Jura, the factories have an obsession with decoration that reaches all the way to invisible parts.

Guilloché is one of the techniques illustrating this effect which has something of both the metronome and the weather vane about it. Many of the parts that go into the movement are engraved with ornamental patterns, using tools that produce subtle and delicate motifs for the eye of the owner.

Colimaçonnage and *soleillage* are two of the spiralling or radiating patterns applied to ratchets, along the edge of bridges and barrels and other mechanical parts that, like the precious supporting cast in a show, are beautiful by virtue of their very attention and restraint.

I

IMPRIMER, PRINTING

When an artisan comes to the table it is not, we can be sure, to claim his lunch. The two tables set out for him here are unique, being nearly 150 metres long, and are used for printing silk scarves. They are like reading tables on which a book consisting of a single page acquiescently and voluptuously stretches out.

Silk twill, then, is the paper here. It is unrolled and stretched like the mock-up in a newspaper office. Covered with glue to keep the silk from moving and the design from getting deformed, it is ready for the laying on of numerous frames.

Like a host of freelancers serving the picture they must evoke, these frames come before the silk one by one, humble yet determined. Printing begins with the *finesse*, the outline, a kind of caption stand that maps out the theme. Then comes the filling, the *rentrures*, working from the smaller to the bigger areas, from dark tones to light. And as these team members speaking in the language of colours come and go, so the design becomes clearer and more precise. It is finished when the *liste* appears, that is, at the edge of the square, the margin in which the "rolling" will occur. Known as "frame-printing" or "Lyonnaise printing", this traditional technique consists of successively printing each colour that constitutes the design of a scarf, frame after frame, in a precise order. Some designs involve as many as forty-six frames. Using this age-old method, it is possible to print one hundred and fifty scarves at once. Cut to the size of a square newspaper page, these *carrés* will soon be daily gazettes worn around necks.

INSCULPER, HALLMARKING

In a flattened lozenge, two initials, E and H (for Emile Hermès) surround a stirrup. This is the maker's hallmark. Gold is identified by an eagle's head, platinum by a dog's, and silver by the head of Minerva. These are the state hallmarks applied by the guarantee offices attached to the French customs authority. Every jewel bears this kind of mark, and has done since the hallmarking of precious metals became obligatory under Napoleon. Were it to be found in dictionaries, which it is not, the term *insculpation* would of course be a close neighbour of *inculpation*. The latter signifies accusing the presumed perpetrator of a felony, the former, wearing its *s* like an official's sash, is a passport to authenticity, a sign of good conduct printed in the precious metal.

INTERPRÉTER, INTERPRETING

If to interpret is to orally translate from one language into another, then the Hermès designers and artistic directors working in the fields of fashion and clothing are supreme linguists. Ever since the 1920s, the house workshops have turned out sports clothes in which function comes before ornament and beauty is born of utility. They have the charm of the essential, and that remains the goal of these polyglot stylists today. In the 1930s, Hermès became the specialist of haute couture knitwear. Dresses in silk bourrette and wild silk, paragons of simplicity, delighted the bohemian instincts of an international clientele. As of the 1960s, the ready-to-wear departments continued the experiment with the noble materials and pared-down forms that defined the house's modernity and freedom from artifice. Budding and established designers served as artistic directors, working to enrich the stylistic vocabulary. Catherine de Karolyi (1967-1978), Nicole de Vésian (1978-1981), Eric Bergère (1981-1989), Claude Brouet, who brought together the designers Christiane Bailly, Myrène de Prémonville, Thomas Maier, Tan Giudicelli, Marc Audibet, Michèle Meunier and Olivier Chatenet (1989-1997), Martin Margiela (1998-2004), Jean Paul Gaultier (2004-2011), and Christophe Lemaire (since 2011) have been the originators of women's collections that nurture reserve and discretion like the oyster its pearl. Bernard Sanz (1986-1988) organised the first show of men's fashion. Since 1989, Véronique Nichanian has brought insight and stylistic independence to the men's collections that she directs, helping to create a style that is natural, poetic and timeless. By faithfully following the inherited Hermès grammar, each has introduced a subtle new set of conjugations, moving seamlessly from interpretation to authorship.

I

LIÉGER, BOARDING

While tanning operations are collective, with skins all sitting together in their various tubs, finishes are applied on an individual, à la carte basis. After the mass drowning, leather recovers its individuality on the workshop tables. The favours it will receive are decided and assessed, then tested and corrected. The pampering that ensues could not even be matched by make-up and manicure specialists working in tandem.
Most bovine leathers are smooth, but there are techniques that can correct their grain, revealing their character with different kinds of relief which change their appearance. In order to obtain boarded leather, for example, the leather is rolled up like a piece of pastry. Originally, this was done by hand using a cork board, the effect of which is to bring the grain to the surface. The form of this grain may vary depending on the direction of the boarding. Like a subtle but ephemeral recipe by a refined cosmetologist, it fades slightly with time, showing the trace of these special treatments. Treated in this way, boarded leather is suited to rigid bags, offering the poise and pride of a face resplendent from a session at the beautician's.

LISSER, GLAZING

When skins are exotic we look indulgently on the kind of artificial cabaret colours that would never be tolerated on bovine leathers. Ostrich and crocodile strut around in accoutrements that would make a dancer at the Lido feel envious and mousy. Twenty-five colours, from extremely arrogant to terribly tender, are permitted. Fuchsia, aniseed, mauve and violet, among these cabaret stars, compete to prove their panache. Tanned and tinted, leather tends to be on the matt side. Just as their relief can be heightened, so can their shine. The leather is rubbed with an agate stone, cut into a cylinder. There is no need even to heat it: the pressure alone produces a temperature of three hundred degrees, which brings out the natural albumen added during the preparation of the skin. Hermès habitually polishes its Box calfskin, while lambskin, emu and crocodile are rubbed with wool felt for a satiny look. Only lizard, and also crocodile, can be glazed using agate stone so as to compete with those glitter-drenched outfits we applaud at night while sipping champagne.

N

1

MACÉRER, MACERATING

Among ideas about fashion, macerating is not a good guest. A lady of taste with a penchant for striking and witty apothegms was holding forth on fashion at the mellow end of the meal. Fashion, she claimed, was not so different from bananas: when overripe it seems adulterated, off the contemporary point; when not ripe enough, too green, hard and new, it fails to catch on. As she savoured the perfectly stewed prunes, she pointed out that fashion and the present coexist in a poetic and mysterious symbiosis: there's no time to simmer gently or correct the seasoning.

In the perfume industry, however, maceration only ennobles. Between three and four weeks, in enormous vats, the concentrate is steeped in alcohol in order to raise it to the height of its olfactive powers, which only the master perfumer can judge. After cooling and filtering, the drops of a limpid perfume can then be stored in bottles and phials, ready to be dabbed on the neck day after day, unconcerned about use-by dates.

MARIER, PAIRING

In the couture workshops, superstitions last longer than fashions, which come unstitched faster than they are sewn. A spilled box of pins heralds a row. Among the hopes and fears maintained amidst the prattle of pinking shears, marriage is a ribbon that is insistently unrolled. It is a preoccupation, a subject of discussion that breaks the silence of the workshop. Some apprentices, who hope for the event, leave a stowaway hair in the hem of a wedding dress being made for another bride. Every year, unmarried workers aged twenty-five celebrate the day of the Catherinettes, still a commonly honoured event in Parisian fashion houses. For this occasion they wear hats whose originality and dexterity display the excellence of their craft. Curiously for this world of luxury that weaves so many dreams, employees of the same firm are advised not to intermarry, for the sake of peace in the workplace. The romance that ends badly is held up in warning like cloves of garlic in Transylvania, though exceptions can be made for those with a solid case.

When it comes to a glove and its better half, marriage is not only discussed without embarrassment but eagerly sought. Silent and docile, these items represent no conjugal risk.

Cutting to the chase, at a simple glance, the glover assembles the most compatible pairs. In the late 1920s, when Hermès started making gloves, first for riding and then for sport, gloves were items that one "paired off". Thanks to the kindly but keen eye of an expert matchmaker who brings together right and left hands, each one is sure to be hand-in-glove with its opposite number.

MATELASSER, CUSHIONING

A saddle comprises five continents, laid out in geographical zones separated by borders of stitching. Between the tree, the seat, the flaps, the girths and the panels the *entente* is *cordiale*, since all are inclined to work together in supporting animal and rider. Cushioning is a technique now used with increasing rarity. Under a piece of fabric stretched over the saddle, the artisan stealthily introduces wool or horsehair which he spreads evenly over the surface using a long awl. For reasons of comfort, the horsehair or wool now tend to be replaced by new materials, such as foam or latex, which have great ergonomic qualities. The landscape of the saddle can thus display its regions, its rounded hillocks and plains, its hollows and slopes, forming a territory unchanged since it was first mapped out, all those decades ago.

METTRE À L'EAU À LA RIVIÈRE, PUTTING IN THE RIVER

As if recently shed, skins are kept in a cold room solemnly maintained at a constant temperature of three degrees. They are then "put in the river". Placed in big vats made of bolondo wood, or *foulons* (drums), which have the advantage of being little affected by wetness, these raw hides undergo several chemical baths, at the end of which they proudly display their new-found solidity, inviolability and elasticity. A ring joins the animal's tail to its head, and keeps the skin from getting in a tangle in its intimidating vat. In a wild impromptu dance where we might recognise, loosely assorted, figures from the world of fashion (here a crocodile press attaché, there a lamb couturier, and over there the ostrich model and manly calfskin photographer), the skins begin their infernal bacchanalia. In this endless eddying, the vats rough-house the skins which pretend to be friendly housemates but in fact are jostling for pole position. This liming (*pelanage*) swells the skins imprisoned in the drums. It helps to dissolve the epidermis, leaving only the dermis. Pickling, done in a mixture of acid and salt water, and tanning, in a bath of chrome, are two more treatments inflicted on these impudent skins. Chrome imparts a blue tint to this strange, constantly moving procession. The "skins are dropped" when, wet and disillusioned by all the fuss and trickery, the drained hides are laid out like a *millefeuille* on a table, exhausted, trusting and promising.

METTRE EN TOURNURE, TURNING UP

A hat is a fashion item. It is also a means of locomotion whose old-fashioned charm recalls the big aeroplanes of yore. On the runway apron or on a peg, this head covering consists of a brim, which has a top side and an under-

side, and a crown. What with these and the sides and the grosgrain or other ribbon, all that needs to be added is perhaps the label which, positioned at the back, indicates both the way it should face and the direction of the wearer's journey.
Mettre en tournure means turning up the edges of a hat's brim, be it a bowler hat or a top hat, in order to sew on the grosgrain, the official ribbon that announces imminent departure.

MONTER, ASSEMBLING

When the scrubbed or humble leather finally arrives on the artisan's table, proud of itself at last, a bag of separated, cut-out bag parts, like a pictogram of the object itself, is methodically laid out.
A Kelly bag, for example, is made by assembling forty different pieces. Each artisan is in charge of making a whole bag, from beginning to end – a traditional practice still honoured today. Thus the craftsman intervenes in an unchanging order of operations. Let us skim quickly past the stages in which lining, inner pockets, the laying of the base, the addition of the metal parts known as "jewellery", all seem only to be delaying the eagerly awaited moment when the bag will be expanded to its full volume. The base is stitched on both sides, front and back. At this stage, the bag is still a travesty of itself because it is perfectly flat, denying its function. Stitched to the body of

the bag, the rigid handle, comprising five different pieces of leather, impatiently suggests its imminent destiny. A shape appears when the artisan assembles the two sides of the bag with the gussets that will give it the model's capaciousness and recognised shape. The tabs for the straps and the swivel clasp are fixed using nails (sixteen of them on a Kelly) whose heads are rendered soft and friendly to the touch by pearling off. Thus kitted out, the bag is ready for the famous little padlock and key-bell. More than any other, a Hermès bag is assembled by hand – by the hand of this artisan who, from beginning to end, from the saddle stitch to the addition of metal parts, joins, stitches and glazes the bag, and also signs it. Each artisan personalises the bag that he has superbly fashioned by discreetly and subtly "imprinting" his signature.

V

I

NOUER, TYING

On staircases and in drawing rooms, in the stores where an accumulation of orange recipients are done up in brown ribbon, you have a fair chance of meeting men and women with a piece of fabric round their neck. Far from being caught in some dutiful or dreary noose, these people are pleasurably bewitched by silk, connoisseurs and addicts of the art of tying ties and scarves and its many variations.

It started in 1949 when Hermès started slipping its neckties around men's collars as a passport to casinos. In woven and then printed silk, pleasure was taken in twisting these accessories and effort was put into renewing their figurative, animal and traditional themes. And since 1937, the house has been known for enfolding, draping, adorning and even warming the long hair and bare skin of women who feel at home in a colourful silk square. Sometimes, even, a foulard is knotted around the handle of a bag like a sophisticated and serpentine reminder. There are more than a hundred ways of tying a scarf, and there are even playing/knotting cards illustrating the multiple ways of disguising this piece of silk as a turban, a giant neck-nesting butterfly or a textile memo. Just as a knot in a handkerchief jogs the memory, so the tying of a scarf captures elegance.

)

)

OURLER, HEMMING

A fashion designer and pioneer of ready-to-wear caused a scandal in the 1960s by showing the stitches in her sweaters. Sonia Rykiel boldly broke with centuries of secret and finished sewing, the backbone of civilian costume. Later, in the 1980s, Japanese designers followed suit. Modern and radical, Yohji Yamamoto and Rei Kawakubo got rid of hems and thanks to them the decade witnessed the reign of the unfinished, the incomplete. Their dresses, like sketches in paint or charcoal, did not end with a neat line.

The stylistic school of Belgian designers made these principles conceptually self-evident. One of its leaders, Martin Margiela, came to work for Hermès. The frayed, the patched, the worn and the dulled were conjoined with excellence and savoir-faire, but without opposition. It was clear to all that the unfinished, no less than the highly finished, was all about dexterity and despised its cack-handed opposite, poor execution.

At Hermès, hemming a man's shirt takes seven stitches per centimetre. That means seven stitches per centimetre of fabric, two more than is usual. These two extra stitches ensure that hems and seams have an elegant, invisible and precious finish, a bespoke solidity. Trivial and fundamental, they are an axis that locates a respect for tradition, engaging modernity while disguising it as a classic.

D

I

PALISSONNER, PULLING AND KNIFING

The tanning and leather workshop sometimes has the look of a beauty parlour. The multiple operations and manipulations to which the pieces of leather are subjected involve these new kinds of client in treatments and protocols that haven't budged an inch. The worker here may not bother with the preciousness of a beautician, but he does share her attachment to the unchanged techniques of the chromatic repertoire. Tanned and dyed, pieces of leather undergo a series of interventions that range from drying to spinning, from massaging to thinning. Goat and sheep skins pass between two rollers that compress but do not curl, coming out lighter and therefore softer. They are then dried, by "exposure to the wind" or in a vacuum. Depending on the degree of suppleness required, the drying will be slow or, if stiffness is the priority, quick. Stretched, moistened and glazed, like relaxed beauty-parlour regulars the skins lend themselves to the massaging and softening sessions. Dry fulling (*foulonnage*) brings out their natural grain. Done by hand, *palissonnage* is the process of pulling and knifing in which a strange semicircular metal blade is applied to render crocodile skins supple. Either process makes a fitting end to this treatment worthy of a wellness centre.

PARER, PARING

To pare is not to parade. It is not to adorn at will. Since for the saddle maker, more often than not, function is the sole ornament, there is no point expecting the job of paring to seek justification in decorative preparations. Rather than showy or pretty artifices, *parer* is a technical process of thinning the edges of leather, sometimes so that it can be folded over and stitched (*remborder*), just like a hem of fine fabric.

This *rembordée* finish is typical of leather work. It is the opposite of what is known as the trimmed, or *rognée* finish, in which the leather is "cut clean," as it is in saddlery. The point of paring is to preserve the material's natural thickness by folding it over itself. To pare is not to heighten but to strive to merge and more effectively conceal. Once again, it is a subtle detail indicative of work in which quality is not a side-effect.

PATINER, PATINATING

Given the overproduction of ideas and objects, the true masterpiece that neither a couturier nor a fashion designer has ever made would consist of composing a collection for life. By this I mean a wardrobe with not much in it but only the best. A short dress with a round neck, a grey flannel skirt, a red sweater, a tuxedo, an evening dress that never over-dresses, men's trousers that really are for men.

In this pictogram of a wardrobe, the bag could only be a Kelly. The older it got, the more unique, the more uniquely hers it would be, like those bags whose leather becomes coloured all the way through from all the knocks and caresses, turning into the everyday mirror of its affectionate owner. Her hand that embrocates it without meaning to executes a form of embroidery that cannot be taught. To appreciate these nuances is to know what *patiner* means.

In the strict sense, as it is used in the workshops, this patinating of a saddle means daubing the leather with vegetable oil. Once dry, it must be rubbed with a moist sponge soaked in soap, making circular movements and maintaining constant if light pressure. *Patiner* means polishing, plushing, ennobling, it is to indicate a life before use. In other places and in other words, it means understanding that fashion is its own poison and its own antidote. It is a threat to those who succumb to its stillborn charm. This incarnation of leather is one way of resisting it.

PERLER, BEADING

Various metal items are pierced, fixed and riveted to the four corners of the leather. Tabs for straps, fastenings and swivel clasps, to name but a few, are fixed by the simple and archaic action of banging on the stud with a hammer. Some fashion houses have made a signature of

aggressive, grouped metal studs that form patterns and accidents. The street has made these visible constellations its own in the form of the messages blazoned over the leather-clad backs of bikers.
Needless to say, there is not even the thin tip of a suggestion of all this at Hermès. The stud favoured here is bare and without arrogance. Austere in itself, it becomes voluptuous by the action known as *beading*. This operation straight from the jewel-setter's book of skills consists in giving the cut tip the same convex, pearl-like appearance as its head. The arid stud, soft to the touch, is a distinguishing sign, which demonstrates belonging to the house. It is the ruse that transforms the mechanic and artisan into a jeweller, all the way.

PLAIRE, PLEASING
In the workshops of couture houses, like those of the establishment that specialises in red leather, when a garment falls from its hanger, it is the custom to say that it will please. If it insists and slips from the iron or wooden shoulders a second time, it is said that it will be bought without hesitation.

PLANER, PLANISHING
In equestrian sports, the French word *planer* – planishing – means to "pass an obstacle horizontally". Much as Hermès loves horses, its use of the verb has nothing to do with riding. Nor does *planer* – commonly meaning to hover –

signify the kind of state in which we lose the sense of reality, like the great dreamers. Quite the contrary, the term is used in the Puiforcat workshops for the craft of silversmithing. A *planeur* uses a whole variety of mallets which are the musical instruments with which he hammers the elements he wants to flatten. *Planage* evens the elements one wishes to shape. To the insistent tap of corrective hammers, the artisan removes humps, accidents and deformations and makes the expanses of metal smoother and more silent than a silver lake.

PLAQUER, GLOSSING UP

The ostrich is unfairly mocked for its lack of courage. The poor bird is too seldom thanked for the access it affords to all kinds of fantasies. In the 1920s, big ostrich-feather fans adorned both the *extravagantes* and the plainly dressed *garçonnes*. On a few exuberant hats one would see the proud plume standing to attention. Today, it is only on stage, in music hall and cabaret, that we see it gathered in tufts around the graceful bodies of half-naked dancers.

Ostrich leather is unmistakeable. The root of the feathers leaves the memory of its ostentation. Roughnesses or follicles writ large, like spikes, punctuate the skins, which need to be lined. Ostrich leather is glossed up using a heated plate (*plaquer*), and hammered. It gains the durability it will need to withstand the sarcasm that is always directed at the ostrich.

PLIER, FOLDING

The seriousness of the tie does not brook mockery or questioning of its status. An immoveable symbol of authority, power, success and convention, the tie is an artifice that performs no function. It adorns. Humble or pretentious, talkative, voluminous or narrow, it belongs among those fashion accessories created to serve appearance, which it annotates with brief commentaries that are plain or colourful. Unlike its friends the fashionable scarf or bag, it never need suffer relegation to the rank of inconsequential frivolities justified only by mood or whim. When a man amasses ties and bowties for his collars, we do not condemn him as a capricious spendthrift as we might others. On its own, the tie's solemnity protects it from all fluctuations of appreciation. From bootlace to kipper, it comprises two parts, a small and a large, assembled and seconded by a lining. To give it greater poise, a second lining, or interlining, is placed inside. According to a special Hermès method, the tie is closed. The special folding that is then applied gives it an exceptional fullness. The silk twill used certainly plays a role in this stylish undertaking. These ties are never solemn like sermons.

PLISSER, PLEATING

However basic, meeting rooms can be the theatre for adventures or happenings. During a working session for a project that never happened, a visibly impatient young woman broke off the attendants' morose maunderings: "Forgive me for interrupting", she said, "the meeting is running so late and I've a child I have to go and fetch, who must be waiting for me in the street." And, with a hint of a southern accent, she added: "Just the thought of it makes my back pleat!" For many of us, this was the first time we had heard such an expression. We were manifestly soothed by the local poetry of her words. Across the table, we hung our linen of manifold thoughts on the line put out by this young woman who had dashed off to get her son. We were all in Marseille and thinking of her pleated back. Was it draped with dread? Was it tanned? Did it see itself as a worried pucker? Other more underhand types turned as she left to see if she wasn't wearing a backless dress. Others, who were amused, imagined what would have happened if she had been wearing a Fortuny dress with its recognisable folds or an Issey Miyake ensemble with small light pleats.

A fabric is no more likely to fall naturally into pleats than a back is to finely fold. Folds are formed by a number of techniques. The simplest one is to form the fold, to sew it, and then to iron it. More permanent are the ones made by tuckers with their strange folding boards, which are like concertina moulds that shape the fabric into the desired zigzag. As for a silk twill scarf of the *plissé* variety, it is mechanically folded in the fabric. Lognon is the house that does this for Hermès on an exclusive basis. A conscientious machine forms the folds one by one. The design becomes more abstract, the scarf seems to grow lighter. In the round box where it can keep all its springiness, it lies ready to act the bodyguard for those with sensitive backs.

POSER UN FILET, ADDING A TRIM

Poser un filet is an intervention that is applied to ceramic and crystal. It is performed at the Hermès workshops at Nontron, where porcelain objects are sandblasted and decorated, or at Saint-Louis. While the term might also translate as "putting down a net", this operation is no riparian hobby, and the fish to fry here are static and fragile and can be broken by the slightest clumsy movement. While they may have some of the same tones and shades as fish scales – the grey of trout or carps, say, or salmon pinks, or the colours of aquarium fish – the glasses, cups, plates and change trays caught by the artisan in his workshop swim more effectively on tables than in freshwater. They have nothing of the sardine or seahorse about them. *Poser un filet* means, quite simply, to add a trim, to delicately apply colours or precious materials (gold or platinum, either matt or shiny) on the edge of a piece, at the top or bottom, using a fine brush that no angler would have in his kit.

PRENDRE DES MESURES,
TAKING MEASUREMENTS

Long after a certain fashion house had closed down, much to its own distress but amidst general indifference, a notebook kept by its founder turned up when her work was being rediscovered. Its stepped pages with their A to Z thumb tabs were covered with methodically written figures, the sign of systematic and almost military order. At the top of each block of numbers, the name of a client was neatly written. These famous or obscure ladies were honoured by the arithmetic portrait that followed, for the rows of numbers were quite simply their measurements: waist, under-bust, bust, hips, arm length (from the neck to the bend of the arm, from neck to wrist), arm, forearm, wrist, etc. Following these rigorously ordered descriptions in centimetres, it was possible to make bespoke clothes for refined and demanding clients, without even seeing them. From Maria Casarès to Marlene Dietrich, from the Countess Thingummy to the Princess Wassername, here were intimate, mathematical portraits of several eras of fashion. The notebook was elevated to the status of conceptual artwork and preserved like a holy relic.

The "Bespoke Shirts" department is similarly attentive, making each tailor a potential portraitist. Clients can hesitate between a stud collar and a mandarin collar, the dandy collar and the Murat collar. In addition to his preferred buttons, he has the choice of colour and font for the monogram that will make his shirt a signed second skin. It takes five hours to make a pattern in brown paper and a model in cloth, then some twelve for the definitive shirt, depending on the kind of cuffs desired, the type of back that is dreamed of, and the kind of pocket and exclusive fabric a fellow wishes to adopt.

PUTOISER

A man with incipient early baldness is said to be taking life too seriously. No description is offered of the hairstyle and hair-state of a man deep in serious work. If he is too anxious, it will be said that his hair is going white. Be that as it may, no one can claim to measure the ambition and professionalism of an artisan by his hair. So much the better, too, because no operation here can be considered minor. No process, short or long, can be taken lightly. A hair, here, is material for a brush.

Putoiser is a word that elicits laughter, a *putois* being a polecat. Originally evoking the smelliness of the brush used to paint porcelain, today it refers to the use of a sponge to harmoniously unify a coloured surface.

The artisan presses and applies the hairs to the surface, repeating the action as often as necessary, until it is as smooth as a bald pate.

P

RACONTER UNE HISTOIRE, TELLING A STORY

One day, an archaeologist of contemporary societies will surely find himself examining Hermès' first silk scarf. Produced in 1937, *Jeu des omnibus et dames blanches* was inspired, both in title and theme, by a board game popular about a hundred years before, at the time when the house was founded. Its soft colours and strongly narrative content, printed using the woodcut technique, evoke a bygone age while introducing the travel theme and aesthetic which, whether animal or mechanical, is a Hermès constant.

Our man in the field would also discover that 1948 was the year the "flat-frame" or "Lyonnaise" method of printing was first used for a silk scarf. This technique affords superior printing quality and, above all, allows a much greater number of drawings and colours to be used on each scarf. Each design has a name, tells a story and bears the signature of the person who created it.

Our passionate researcher will discover an inventory with a wealth of over two thousand scarf designs made since the early days, produced at a rate of thirty-five new models each year. Each design tells a new story often related to the theme chosen for the year of its production.

In these picture puzzles on silk, attentive readers will find confirmation of a noble artifice whose vocation as a subtle storyteller meant it could never be dismissed as yet another vain object.

RAPPORTER, REINFORCING

"Rapporter un coin" – literally, bring back a corner – is not the title of some bit of Dadaist theatre with sardonic japes in place of narrative, nor does it mean bringing back a patch of paradise or some other spot as a souvenir. Nor is it the title of a piece of pulp fiction or navel-gazing art house film. It is not the summary of a debriefing session or an act of censorship.
So what is it? Strengthening cowhide, making a groove in it to facilitate folding and shaping, and hand-sewing it over poplar wood to make a Hermès trunk: that is what "rapporter un coin" means.

REFENDRE, SPLITTING

The skins are waiting in the antechamber, patient and silent like blank sheets of paper. On rows and rows of metal shelves they are neatly arranged by colour and shade. Were it not for the variable, wild contours of each piece of leather, you'd think you were in a stationer's store room, where large-format sheets of paper were waiting to be cut. Here the leather looks like blotting paper. Slicker than the pages of a magazine without a subject, other leathers packed in close ranks shine in the artificial light. Plain or sophisticated, the pages are at rest, evoking a giant, fragmented and naked book.

Among the many operations that skins undergo, splitting is the one that most merits the analogy with paper. Very popular in the 1930s, the technique consists in splitting the leather horizontally using a blade or a machine. Thus slimmed, discreet, svelte and distinguished, these finer pieces of leather are free to settle into desk blotters and cultivate new affinities.

REMMAILLER, LINKING

The *clothes clinics* that were once such a fixture on our city streets have all disappeared. They were places where you could take the holed elbows of a beloved pullover you refused to abandon, or the nick in the knee of some favourite trousers. Each darning stitch, each patch added in these sartorial sanatoria were a homage to worn clothes. A place where they would be given a new lease on life. Rather than patch up, darn or mend, it is said, we now prefer to throw away. Rather than carefully look after the old, goes the argument, we have chosen the new for the sake of the new, until death do us – from taste and desire – part.

Remmailler is the opposite of *chamailler* (to bicker). In some cases, it is a matter of repairing, as when knitwear has picked holes in itself and needs to cover them up. In other cases, it is a matter of joining two pieces, fabric and knit, while avoiding surplus threads or whipping, that additional thickness or those stitches that make the result inelegant. On a loom that looks like a Mohican haircut made of metal needles, the edge of a sleeve, a collar or panel of knitting is joined with a piece of material that has already been perforated, such as crocodile or mink. *Remmailler* is a virtuoso technique, the hallmark of the finest houses. A *remmailleuse* is a woman – or a machine – who harmoniously marries two incompatible individuals. The garments and accessories brought into being by her fingers – or its needles – are both hybrid and natural, without breaks or tears. It is our responsibility to watch over this technical prodigy and preserve it with the care of a clothes doctor.

RÉPARER, REPAIRING

A cotton tank top, once known as a "skin knit," was constellated with awkward embroideries that turned nicks on the bust into a starry sky. A mechanic's overalls had been so often mended that the robust piece of fabric was a monument to the man who had worn it all his life. An austerely cut skirt accumulated levels under its multicoloured variety of remnants, like the strata of a precious and slowly forming landscape. All these clothes from the early twentieth century, now to be found in modern collections, belonged to modest men and women. Frequent mending and careful ironing have made them as sophisticated as the haute couture models fought over at auction.

After the 1960s, fashion added the words *disposable* and *throwaway* to its diabolical vocabulary: consumption had to be kept going, its momentum maintained. The intimate relations, lasting longer than a season, that we all develop with one or more items in our wardrobe, are not deemed of interest here. Our attachment to apparel is not to its liking. It has won the battle, if not the war. It has instituted the reign of the disposable and the short-term.

Hermès sees things differently. Every client can bring back favourite objects to be repaired in a dedicated workshop. More painstaking than a *remmailleuse* delicately joining knitted fabric and other materials at the turn of the last century, the men and women here change and dress these pieces, recreating their lost colours and swearing that they will last as long as fashion is fashion.

REPOUSSER, EMBOSSING

At Puiforcat, beakers and pitchers, coffee pots and tea pots are all subjected to the same treatment when it comes to creating the curves that enhance the style of hollow ware and round vessels. On a piece of wood or metal, a mandrel that itself has the curves of a strutting beauty, shapes are hammered into a sheet of silver using a tool called a "spoon" (*cuillère*). The process must be repeated several times, and the object annealed more than once, for the piece to attain the perfect curve that will be deemed as feminine as a petticoat in the case of a teapot and as virile as a puffed-out chest in the case of pitchers. Annealing is the operation that consists in passing the piece over a flame and then under cold water to make the metal more supple. Dimpled like an infant, stooped like an elegant elderly lady, chubby like a provincial man of standing, these patiently hammered pieces come slowly to life as they imitate the plump model put before them like an unbreakable mirror.

RETIRER L'ÉCAILLE, REMOVING THE SCALE

John Lobb, lover of bespoke shoes, would be surprised to hear of people "removing the scales". Now, this is not some fish recipe shared by enthusiastic cooks, nor, some erotic-poetic fantasy about undressing a mermaid. The scale removed here is in fact a thickness of wood on the model being carved to imitate the client's foot. On paper, the last maker takes down the measurements of the client's feet twice, first when seated, then when standing. These metrics are then used to sculpt a last in hornbeam, a wood that is little affected by variations in humidity. The shoe is built around this wooden last sculpted in the course of the client's fitting sessions. The quarters are carefully shaped and the last smoothed with a file.

Further work brings the waist to the required definition, and, when the artisan with his file brings the last to an almost perfect copy of the client's foot, this is called "cleaning the articulation". When he removes less than a millimetre of thickness, it is also said that he is "removing the scale," which is a way of pointing out that at John Lobb, made-to-measure really is measured down to the nearest scintilla.

RETOURNER, TURNING INSIDE OUT

When a bag is finished, it must be turned inside out, like a glove on an unknown hand. A kind of soft sculpture that only acquires its final volume by inversion, without going through the phase of casting (here, it is the stitching that provides the armature, the skeleton), a bag reveals its true nature during this slow and painstaking handling. Centimetre after centimetre, the leather is treated with infinite dignity and tact, never forced or handled abruptly or brutally. This is exactly how a plastic surgeon or dermatologist would go about his work, except that the craftsman uses no artificial fillings to achieve his goal. He starts by turning up the corners with his friendly fingers, then gently rolls the leather until, docile and trusting, it submits. Supple, malleable and flighty leathers – *Swift*, *Clémence*, *Togo* for a start, and other prouder, more stubborn customers, such as *Box* – all go through the same exercise which, if certainly sophisticated, sometimes requires impressive strength as well, especially with the larger pieces. After this shape-setting session which seems to transform the artisan into a medium whose predictions are uncertain, the bag's form is further refined by gentle hammer blows to the piping along the edges. The artisan is all concentration, listening carefully as he taps with his hammer. In response to this Morse code whose purpose and meaning only he understands, the bag becomes all titivated, but with grace, determination and gravitas. A gentle session with the steam iron, applied as quickly and daintily as to chiffon, removes all the traces of this handling which is nothing to blush about. Now it is up to its future companions never to put it directly on the floor: that, they say, will drive away the household's earnings!

RÉTREINDRE, SWAGING

Anyone familiar with French will surely be tempted to place *rétreindre* in the same family as *étreindre*, a verb that promises embraces of all kinds, from enlacing and entwining to pressing and squeezing. Such a touchy-feely free-for-all would, were it not for the weight of the bodies involved, be at home in the airy exaltation of love poetry. But no, *rétreindre* is not some kind of second bite at the cherry of hugging – sad, perhaps, but true. To witness this process you will have to try the silver and gold workshops.

Having pencilled in the guidelines and construction plans of an object on a plaque, the smith cuts it out and hammers it with bevelled mallets, always following the same trajectory, from the centre out to the edges. A blow must never hit the same spot twice. The whole point of swaging is to "lead the metal". The weight of the blows must be constant, in order to attain the same thickness throughout the piece, in the round parts and in the flat parts of concave items such as soup bowls and sauce boats, for which swaging is tantamount to regular modelling.

ROULOTTER, ROLLING

Window displays are still lifes whose slumped actors plead silently with passers-by to "get me out of here". Some textile items proclaim proudly to passers-by, "Hand-rolled, I am hand-rolled!" The visitor in the street will respond to this delicate attention, this mute claim. She sees it as an invisible added value, an early manifestation of the distinction soon to be hers. A flurry of scarves disdain the raw edge, that precipice to vulgarity. Ties in moods of many colours collapse with shame on their bellies at the very thought of losing their rolled singularity. Dress hems, swooning at the thought of the ankles they will soon swish against, grow tense under the agile fingers of a specialist seamstress. *Roulotter* – to roll – is to cosset a hem. It is to make an addition with two nimble fingers, an addition not made to be seen. It is doing without showing what one has done. A rolled edge whispers more than it shouts its difference. With a running stitch of silk thread, the roll is executed like a hushed conversation reaching its amicable end. Ensuring that the stitches are never visible, the *roulotteuses* roll the disciplined hem on the front side, from the edge inwards. These artisans spend months learning their gentle movements and disdainfully reject the use of an iron.

When a foulard, scarf or tie settles naturally on a shelf, its edges curled by meticulousness and time, and whisper "hand-rolled", do please let them nestle about your neck. When the wind blows, when their tips fly up in your face, who knows, you may still feel the precious fingers that so discreetly drummed on them.

S

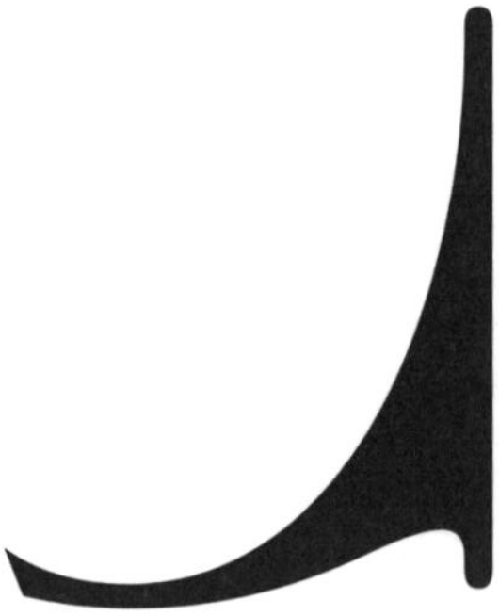

SABLER, SANDBLASTING

In the Hermès workshop at Nontron, in the Périgord, everything centres around tableware and table decoration. Here, a simple Siamese handle, a saucer that many would find ordinary and a spout that is anything but voluble are treated with the same esteem as a laboratory researcher. The quality of the ceramic could warrant a thesis, a shade of white a university dissertation. Among the sophisticated, archaic or high-tech procedures and techniques taught here, we find *sablage* – sandblasting – in which powerful jets of sand, more precise than a calligrapher's brush, are used to engrave motifs figurative or abstract, mathematical or naïve, on porcelain. The sand lifts the fine outer layer of enamel to reveal the raw ceramic, or "biscuit". The design in polished relief, the curves and accents educated by the directional grains of sand fashion cups and whole table services whose soft, mysterious feel is something that cannot be taught.

SABRER, BURRING

It is said that when one of Madeleine Vionnet's workers flew into a fit of pique after a heated exchange of views she picked up a pair of pincers and mechanically "pillaged" the velvet of the dress she was working on. With abrupt, tense movements, she pulled up threads, singly or in tufts, creating gaps in the different depths of fabric. The couturière, so the story goes, was delighted and asked her to do it again, but in a more organised way, which is how a dress in hand-devoured red velvet bloomed with solid modernist roses and the memory of a spat that took a turn for the better.

If burring a fabric is not exactly the same technique, the aim is identical. Vionnet's worker plucked the surface, whereas burring a piece of duchesse satin is a matter of sliding a fine knife into the fibres on the surface, raising and cutting them and making them spread and rise up in contrast with the flatness of the fabric preserved elsewhere. The *float* of the satin obtained by thus breaking the threads acquires the virtues of velvet. The act, *sabrer*, or burring, summons motifs to the printed or plain surface. After that, using a boar's hair brush, one pushes against the pile on a table heated to seventy-five degrees. *Sabrer* is a matter of wounding and breaking, just as the worker chez Vionnet tore and plucked at the fabric.

In half tones, like damask, reserves are employed to unreservedly reveal motifs that are slow, meticulous, and chatty but never loud.

In both cases, the idea is to impart a different tone to the tone, a new meaning that does not clash. It is an alternative opinion but not a spat.

SERTIR, SETTING

To set is to fix a precious stone in a bezel or a mount, folding its edge around the stone. There are several different ways of setting, appreciated for their plastic qualities or the tenacity with which they grip stones that are rarer than the apple of our eye. The prong setting involves metal prongs coming out of the mount and folded back like a hook anxious to keep its beauteous catch. The closed setting encircles the stone with a border that keeps it walled up within itself. The bead setting hammers the stone into a volume of metal from which it cannot escape. The channel setting positions the stones in a line like locomotives between two rails. The rare moustache or shaving setting traps the stone in a hole and then blocks it with a shaving. More common, the burnish setting discreetly pushes and folds the metal around stones laid out in a pavé.

Let us be quite clear: the different ways of setting are not portraits of the mindset of jealous and possessive husbands. Held in its silver claws or metal walls, the stone, insecure because precious, rare and unique, confesses to the reality of fugacity suspended.

SIGNER, SIGNING

In the eighteenth century, honours were showered upon the supplier. He was credited with the creative power that today is the prerogative of the demiurge designer. An embroiderer or weaver was more esteemed than a tailor. What made a garment new was its embroidery, its motifs. The assembly of the different parts by the tailor was one of the final stages of the process. The forms were considered stable. For some makers of fabrics and embroiderers, a distinctive style was not their only signature: sometimes, a seal or initials might appear along the selvedge. In the nineteenth century, milliners and other makers of hats, weary of being asked to alter models that were not of their design or workshop, began to slip labels bearing their house sign inside their headwear. These were the first known company identities. Charles Frederick Worth, the inventor of haute couture in the late nineteenth century, placed his signature on the waist ribbons of his dresses. The long, slanting handwritten letters that composed his name thus labelled the models of the man who soon became known as the "dress artist". Up until the 1920s, only a monogram with the client's initials was tolerated. To schizophrenically wear another person's alphabet was unthinkable. Madeleine Vionnet justified the label in terms of control and prestige, as a means of fighting against the plagiarists. Jean Patou and Chanel did a lot for the use of the logo as visual effect and icon. The less said the better about its excessive, abusive use in the second half of the twentieth century.

At Hermès, to sign is to attest. It is not some simian copy. Hermès. Paris. Made in France.

This is not a label or a mark, but an unchanged hallmark, a satisfied acknowledgement of the work accomplished.

SORTIR AVEC LE BLUES, COMING OUT WITH THE BLUES

One future prospect for the industries of fashion and appearance would be to break with the habit of speeded-up and repeated seasonality, a commercial ploy that is now even less uncertain than the weather.

We need to dream around new principles that renew not only design but the way it is disseminated and produced, its life cycle. We need to encourage parallel paths and pauses for rest, to be able to wax lyrical at a single dress created by a couturier, the result of endlessly cancelled and corrected stylistic subtractions that make it an eternal classic. Soon we should be applauding the creator of a unique collection that is the condensation of twentieth century sartorial archetypes. A designer who strives to cut out all excess or creative abscess, in order to regain a simplicity close to that of traditional clothes, will have progressed even further. As we consider our practices, we will be pleased to imagine the couturier of our moods. An ink-coloured outfit for a gloomy look, a sky-blue shirt for a burst of joy, a neutral grey sweater for greater reserve, etc. Fashion rarely heeds the thoughts of those who wear it and is unaware that when it is not an addiction it can be a medicine.

When clothes flee the pages of magazines, when they run from shops and settle in our wardrobes, it is not only enthusiasm that makes us wear them, but also our mood that morning. There is no moods department in the department stores, or at business schools. Yet mood is more decisive and variable than it is vain.

In the Hermès tanneries in Louisiana, they say that skins "come out with the blues". This may not have anything to do with depression, but let us allow that there is a hint of melancholy in them, under that blue colour they wear.

For it is the mineral tanning process that imbibes skins with melancholia! They are plunged into wave baths and stay there, like absent figures, for twenty-four hours as the temperature rises from twenty-two to thirty-two degrees. Then they rest in a still bath, from which they "come out with the blues", which is normal, given the tinge imparted by the mineral salts they have soaked in.

But no worries. The next phases, colouring and finishing, will be more than enough to convert the blues into something a lot more up-tempo.

SOUFFLER, BLOWING

The delicate glasses made at Saint-Louis are all unique, because they are hand-blown. After meticulous preparation, the blower places the viscous mass of liquid crystal in a mould, then bestows its shape with his breath and the movements of his hands and arms. Like limpid prisoners, his whisperings, his invisible thoughts, his trembling breath are the decorative, silent reveries to which we must lend an ear when we raise our glass.

Γ

TAILLER, CUTTING

The cutting activity in the workshops at Cristalleries Saint-Louis is much closer to fashioning organza and chiffon than to carving stone in a sculptor's studio. Fragility is the opposite of bulk. For many of these cutting actions, the eye is sole judge, dispensing with the painstaking process of tracing out the marks indicating the heights and divisions for the desired motif. In sandstone, or tipped with diamonds, the grinding and cutting wheels enter into a constructivist and precise dance that is both abrasive and delicate. Lace, bevel or diamond cuts and flat, faceted or festooned sides constitute the basic vocabulary in this art of delicate drawing in which the cutter is a choreographer.

TANNER, TANNING

When it reaches the tannery an animal skin is wet, salty, smelly, heavy and sometimes flecked with hair and bits of flesh. Tanning is an essential part of the process that transforms the raw skin into supple and imputrescible leather. It involves four artisanal and very modern stages: the "river process" cleans and prepares the skin. Here, fleshing and unhairing do away with the remaining bits of hair and wool. The epidermis is bloated with water and smooth. Tanning

sensu stricto is the action that makes the leather rot-proof by means of stabilisation products. Vegetable tanning, using bark, wood, roots, leaves and fruits, is the oldest technique. It imparts a visible lustre to the leather, which spends months soaking in tannins of vegetable origin. Mineral tanning, done in drums, is faster. Here, instead of tannins, it is chrome that bestows suppleness and strength.
Colouring and finishing are the final steps that make the skin ready for the leather-goods and saddle workshops.

TEINDRE, DYEING

Beige, dull or bluish-grey when they emerge from the tanning process (vegetable or mineral baths produced different tones), the skins that reach the colouring stage (even the ones to be given a natural look) are in need of perking up. They are plunged into euphoric baths of colour inside cosmic drums. Dyeing and rinsing take a good ten hours, and after this dance the skins emerge soaked, scrubbed, waxed and coloured through and through. And since the spread of the pigments is sometimes uneven, some skins are treated to a little extra surface colouring. The shades, all three hundred of them, are the result of precise formulae, some of them very old, which are kept preciously on a sheet that is like their chromatic pedigree. One hundred and twenty constant colours are listed for some thirty different kinds of leather.

The skin itself adds its own hue to the natural or contrived colour attributed to it, thus further enriching the basic spectrum. While exotic skins daringly sport extravagant and sharp Pop tones, natural cowhide comes only in – yes – natural. Calfskin, taurillon, goatskin and lamb go into carnival mode in over thirty shades. The finishing operations add sophistication to the epidermis, heighten the relief and grain, and give added depth to the colours. Whatever the final hue, Hermès is adamant that it should fully express the characteristics of the skin. As with a human face, colour is like make-up that enhances but never masks its prized natural distinction.

TISSER, WEAVING

For many, and not only fashionistas with a pronounced lack of interest in geometry, a square – a *carré* – is essentially a piece of fabric, a silent archetype that silkily intimates its origin just by being there. Hermès *carrés* can be recognised at once by their colours and rich, varied drawings ranging from cornucopian to rigorous, and by their contemporary or old-fashioned charm. They are also distinguished by the quality of their silk, at once strong and soft. This comes from a Brazilian mill that supplies skeins to Les Tissages Perrin, weaver to Hermès for over half a century. It takes three months to get from the arrival of the raw thread to the rolling of the bolts of domesticated silk twill. Three months for three operations: winding the skeins of raw silk, weaving them into twill with its distinctive diagonal ribs, and degumming, which consists in washing the fabric in order to dissolve the sericin, a kind of natural glue secreted by the silk worm. Now, do those elegant ladies know that the scarf around their neck with its equestrian, floral or other design is the product of no less than four hundred and fifty thousand metres of silk thread?

TRANSMETTRE, PASSING ON

For many houses, their oral or material heritage is like a shiny old peg made of precious wood on which they can hang their good intentions, rather than a support for knowledge and techniques.

Not so with Hermès. Whether in the form of basic and fundamental archives, or the records of a *métier*, its heritage is very much alive. Yesterday's messages are just as eloquent as today's words. Not that the conduct of future generations is dictated by any written guide or log book. Their path must be navigated by hand.

At rue du Faubourg-Saint-Honoré, tradition and its transmission are oral. Digressions and nuances are appreciated, for both preserve the poetry of the work. The tool and execution are the plumb lines of the stories told.

This process of perpetuation is the house's watermark. From generation to generation, a scarf or bag is handed down from mother to daughter. In a workshop, likewise, tools are handed on from artisan to apprentice. Transmission has itself become a precious material. Witness the much-loved cashier who served the house for thirty years, and who left the bag in which she put the day's takings to the Emile Hermès Collection. Patched up all over, and beautiful precisely because of all the mending, it had traversed the history of Hermès like a talisman until the 1970s. Every evening after work, the relic was thrown from hand to hand, for, according to the cashier, it was a failsafe lucky charm, a guarantee of the house's success.

This sainted reticule is now carefully preserved. Held by a wide, protective band, it continues to be appreciated and touched.

TRÉFILER, PULLING AND DRAWING

Tréfiler has the sound of those deep-sea denizens that live down where the light cannot reach. Gide describes them in *The Counterfeiters*, in words reported by Vincent and taken up by the Comte de Passavant: "[…] animals that were blind, it was thought. What use would the sense of sight be in the dark? […] And at last it was discovered that each of these animals which people at first insisted were creatures of darkness, gives forth and projects before and around it its own light. Each of them shines, illuminates, irradiates. When they were

brought up from the depths at night and turned out on to the ship's deck, the darkness blazed. Moving, many-coloured fires, glowing, vibrating, changing – revolving beacon lamps – sparkling of spars and jewels – a spectacle, say those who saw it, of unparalleled splendour."[9]
In jewellery, *tréfiler* means drawing certain metals, cold. They are transformed into wire by passing them through the holds of various draw plates (*filières*). These draw plates are sheets of metal pierced with holes of decreasing diameters, through which bright, sparkling gold, silver and copper wire is passed and thinned.

TRESSER, BRAIDING

If we bear in mind that the horse is Hermès' first client, we will hardly be surprised to see equestrian vocabulary adapting so naturally and fluently to the worlds of men's and women's fashion. And the contrary is also the case, reflecting the esteem in which this noble animal is held.
All Hermès artisans make daily use of this lexicon in which a trot can become a pair of earrings, a saddle decoration a jewel, and equestrian straps the ingredients of the famous *haut à courroie* handbag!

9. André Gide, *Les Faux-Monnayeurs*, Paris, Gallimard, 1925. Dorothy Bussy, Knopf, 1927, *The Counterfeiters*, Vintage Books edition, 1973, p. 152.

The horse is everywhere, pampered like a beloved friend whose well-thumbed photo is kept preciously in a wallet, close to our heart. A host of anecdotes illustrate the role of the horse at Hermès. It is the supreme expression of the house's legitimacy, free of mannerism or fantasy. It stands for respect, starting with the quiet respect with which it is itself treated.

Thus, however extensive the range of leathers it may use, Hermès would never include a skin from a horse, not even an old nag. This is a principle and a motto.

There are of course endless parallels between a human head of hair and a mane. In French, the word for dress, *robe*, is also used for a horse's hair – as if the designer's creation aspired to the perfection of the animal's *coat*.

It is the same thing with braiding – *tresser*. The verb is shared between hairdressers and the world of the racecourse. Humans, as we know, like to braid their hair. And so it goes too for the manes and tails of horses, especially for festive occasions, special outings and competitions. But this way with hair also has other practical, aesthetic aspects. Fine strips of goatskin, braids, are assembled and interwoven in large quantities, flat or round, to make solid watchstraps, belts, crops or even necklaces.

The house has even acquired a machine especially for this purpose. When it comes to braiding, it is the mane attraction.

VAPORISER, SPRAYING

An Englishman who had retired from London was living like a hermit not far from Paris, in an old-fashioned French town suspended in time. About his only known social activity was the occasional lunch with a centenarian seamstress, a respectable old lady who kept a herd of nonchalant kangaroos. At a meal with several other guests, he unselfconsciously brought up the methodical regimen of care he applied to his clothes. He had an exhaustive memory of each garment, having reduced to the bare minimum the extravagance of a wardrobe built around a score of identical suits ordered from Savile Row.

In each one he placed a card, the same size as the inner pocket. Rather as others might stow a precious banknote. On this he scrupulously noted the date of each brushing and visit to the cleaners.

His fellow diners, sharing our period's obsession with hygiene, dismissed the form of avarice attested by this dry cleaning journal as the foible of an old bachelor. Sensing the discomfort in their silence, he cannily replied that elegance was next to parsimony and economy, and quoted Aragon's *Aurélien*: "Just as a suit that has been worn in or a suitcase that has already travelled are in better taste, and more surely pleasurable, than a suit straight from the tailor or a suitcase out of the store, people with a well-stocked wardrobe always look down on those whose clothes are too new."

He was a dandy whose sartorial neutrality was definitive and sublime. In order to more effectively preserve the suits purchased a few years before, the dandy travelled little, was sparing in his movements. What's more, as might be expected, he was a man of great culture, more knowledgeable than all those around the table, who suddenly started looking like an assembly of clothes in bundles, like old rags hanging from a clothesline.

This story, bearing no obvious relation to the theme that detains us here, suggest that, if we can appreciate the action of the dandy, then we may also appreciate the action of spraying a hat. And, consequently, we may grow more deferential towards the contents of our cupboards.

A Motsch felt hat as sold in the store is round and looks like a melon. To give it the sculptural quality for which it is known, it needs to be sprayed using a machine. Some clients remember this and readily revive their hat with a delicately directed cloud of steam.

Several times a day, especially in the months of November and December, when the wind blows, the operation is repeated in the store. As Dadaist as it is essential, it is the memory-under-a-cloche of refined persons.

VISITER, VISITING

Twill scarves fresh from the workshops are like cards, visiting cards from the house of Hermès. Like an impeccably turned out couturier, they must appear "more groomed than a poodle". To ensure that the piece of cut silk is in all ways above reproach, a *visiteuse* examines and touches, then validates or rejects.

At each stage of production, the quality of the *carré* comes under the microscope. No flaw is allowed, not even imperceptible ones. The ultimate stage of this control is called the "visit". More stringent than all other inspections, it sanctions the imprudent scarf, the bohemian foulard with its costly defects, and verifies the behaviour of a motif and its execution.

After this microscopic inspection, the scarf can head for store drawers and appeal to the indulgent necks that it will lavish with fashion and attention.

INDEX

Abat-carrer 13
Arrêter. Stopping 14
Astiquer. Polishing 15
Bichonner. Cleaning and dressing 19
Broder. Embroidering 20
Cadrer une peau. Framing a skin 25
Chipoter. Quibbling 26
Cirer. Waxing 27
Ciseler. Chasing 28
Collectionner. Collecting 29
Colorer. Colouring 30
Composer. Composing 31
Consigner. Recording 32
Coucher les fonds. Laying the ground 33
Coudre. Stitching 34
Couper. Cutting 35
Créer une complication. Creating a complication 37
Cueiller 39
Décomposer. Breaking down 43
Décreuser. Degumming 44
Demander. Request 46
Dessiner. Drawing 46
Donner sa main. Giving handle 48
Doubler. Lining 49
Dresser. Laying-off 51
Empaqueter. Packaging 55
Ennoblir. Ennobling 56
Estampiller. Stamping 57
Etirer. Stretching 57
Façonner 61
Fermer. Fastening 61
Feuilleter. Leafing through 63
Feutrer. Rubbing with felt 64
Fondre. Casting 65
Frapper – Dorer sur cuir. Printing – Gilding leather 66
Gainer. Casing 71
Glacer. Glazing 72
Gratte-bosser. Bump-scratching 73
Graver. Engraving 74
Griffer. Marking 75
Guillocher. Checkering 76
Imprimer. Printing 81
Insculper. Hallmarking 82
Interpréter. Interpreting 82
Liéger. Boarding 87
Lisser. Glazing 87
Macérer. Macerating 91
Marier. Pairing 91
Matelasser. Cushioning 93
Mettre à l'eau à la rivière. Putting in the river 93

Mettre en tournure. Turning up 94
Monter. Assembling 95
Nouer. Tying 99
Ourler. Hemming 103
Palissonner. Pulling and knifing 107
Parer. Paring 108
Patiner. Patinating 108
Perler. Beading 109
Plaire. Pleasing 110
Planer. Planishing 110
Plaquer. Glossing up 111
Plier. Folding 112
Plisser. Pleating 112
Poser un filet. Adding a trim 114
Prendre des mesures. Taking measurements 115
Putoiser 116
Raconter une histoire. Telling a story 119
Rapporter. Reinforcing 120
Refendre. Splitting 120
Remmailler. Linking 121
Réparer. Repairing 122
Repousser. Embossing 123
Retirer l'écaille. Removing the scale 124
Retourner. Turning inside out 125
Rétreindre. Swaging 126
Roulotter. Rolling 127
Sabler. Sandblasting 131
Sabrer. Burring 131
Sertir. Setting 133
Signer. Signing 133
Sortir avec le blues. Coming out with the blues 135
Souffler. Blowing 136
Tailler. Cutting 141
Tanner. Tanning 141
Teindre. Dyeing 142
Tisser. Weaving 143
Transmettre. Passing on 144
Tréfiler. Pulling and drawing 145
Tresser. Braiding 146
Vaporiser. Spraying 151
Visiter. Visiting 153

Our heartfelt thanks to all the teams at Hermès,
John Lobb, Puiforcat and Saint-Louis for their invaluable
and painstaking technical help.
The author would also like to take this opportunity
to express his personal gratitude to Marie-Ange Bernieri
and Alexandre Samson.

The original edition of this book was published in France by Actes Sud, Arles, in collaboration with Hermès.

7 000 copies of this book have been printed in English. A limited English edition of 100 copies, numbered 1 to 100, has also been printed.

GRAPHIC DESIGN: Raphaëlle Pinoncély
PRODUCTION: Géraldine Lay
TRANSLATED from the French by Charles Penwarden
COPY EDITOR: Caroline Taylor-Bouché

Printed in February 2012 by Artegrafica, Verona, Italy, on Old Mill Bianco / Fedrigoni on behalf of Actes Sud, Le Méjan, place Nina-Berberova, 13200 Arles.

ISBN 978-2-330-00275-6
First edition: March 2012
www.actes-sud.fr